VIRTUE

CASCADE COMPANIONS

The Christian theological tradition provides an embarrassment of riches: from Scripture to modern scholarship, we are blessed with a vast and complex theological inheritance. And yet this feast of traditional riches is too frequently inaccessible to the general reader.

The Cascade Companions series addresses the challenge by publishing books that combine academic rigor with broad appeal and readability. They aim to introduce nonspecialist readers to that vital storehouse of authors, documents, themes, histories, arguments, and movements that comprise this heritage with brief yet compelling volumes.

TITLES IN THIS SERIES:

VIRTUE

An Introduction to Theory and Practice

OLLI-PEKKA VAINIO

CASCADE *Books* • Eugene, Oregon

VIRTUE
An Introduction to Theory and Practice

Cascade Companions 29

Cascade Books
An Imprint of Wipf and Stock Publishers
199 W. 8th Ave., Suite 3
Eugene, OR 97401

www.wipfandstock.com

PAPERBACK ISBN: 978-1-4982-3750-5
HARDCOVER ISBN: 978-1-4982-3752-9
EBOOK ISBN: 978-1-4982-3751-2

Cataloguing-in-Publication data:

Names: Vainio, Olli-Pekka.

Title: Virtue : an introduction to theory and practice / Olli-Pekka Vainio.

Description: Eugene, OR : Cascade Books, 2016 | Cascade Companions 29 | Includes bibliographical references.

Identifiers: ISBN 978-1-4982-3750-5 (paperback) | ISBN 978-1-4982-3752-9 (hardcover) | ISBN 978-1-4982-3751-2 (ebook)

Subjects: LCSH: Ethics, Ancient. | Virtue—History. | Prudence—History.

Classification: BJ171.V55 2016 (paperback) | BJ171.V55 (ebook)

Manufactured in the U.S.A.   10/17/16

CONTENTS

ACKNOWLEDGMENTS

THE WORD *VIRTUE* DOES not necessarily have only a positive ring to it. Oftentimes being "virtuous" can be understood in the sense of being simple, having a holier-than-thou attitude, or pretending to be something other than one really is. Simultaneously, we desire that we be treated equally and fairly, and when we fail, we want to be forgiven for our misdeeds and loved unconditionally. We both love virtue and wish to keep it at arm's length. Virtue both makes us sick and cures us.

Defined simply, virtue is a valuable character trait that helps one to achieve a laudable goal in one's life, gain knowledge, or perform a morally excellent deed. Virtue theories are discussed in several spheres of human life, such as in psychology, philosophy, theology, and politics. Outside purely academic circles, virtues are often discussed in self-help literature and in leadership manuals.

This short book will offer an overview of the history of virtues and the basic questions in contemporary conversation. The first chapter looks at the crucial terminological issues and problems in recent discussion. The second chapter focuses on the history of Western philosophy and how virtues have been assessed in various ways over the years. The third chapter presents a short summary of classical virtues. The final chapter discusses some of the applications of virtue theories in epistemology, ethics, psychology, and politics.

The book is based on my Finnish book on virtues, which was supported by the Society of Non-fiction Writers. The Faculty of Theology (University of Helsinki) also supported the translation of this work. Jason Lepojärvi, Timo Nisula, Emilia Lahti, Andrew Pinsent, and Joona Salminen commented on my work and helped me to improve it. Simon Howard corrected my English and translated most of this book. I am grateful to all of them.

ABBREVIATIONS

1

WHAT IS VIRTUE?

FROM THE BEGINNING OF history and within practically all known cultures, we have observed human behavior in terms of virtue. The various virtue traditions have a lot in common, but they also differ from each other. Philosophers and scholars have even severely criticized each other's theories of virtue. In this chapter we will look at definitions of virtues, their history, and key themes in current debate, such as whether it is really possible to be virtuous.

A GENERAL DEFINITION OF VIRTUE

Virtue typically refers to a character trait that expresses some sort of excellence.[1] This is what is meant by the Greek concept *arete*. Generally, the crucial feature of virtue is that it is a mean between two extremes, lack and excess. For example, a person is brave when she behaves neither cowardly

1. A good basic introduction to virtue theory is Austin & Geivett, *Being Good*. Advanced treatments are: Adams, *A Theory of Virtue*; Timpe & Boyd, *Virtues and Their Vices*.

nor foolhardily. Finding the mean is often very hard, and this ability, which Aristotle calls practical wisdom (*phronesis*) is learned through experience alone.

> What has been said is confirmed by the fact that, while young men become geometricians and mathematicians and wise in matters like these, it is thought that a young man of practical wisdom cannot be found. The cause is that such wisdom is concerned not only with universals but with particulars, which become familiar from experience, but a young man has no experience, for it is length of time that gives experience; indeed one might ask this question too, why a boy may become a mathematician, but not a philosopher or a physicist. It is because the objects of mathematics exist by abstraction, while the first principles of these other subjects come from experience, and because young men have no conviction about the latter but merely use the proper language, while the essence of mathematical objects is plain enough to them. . . That practical wisdom is not scientific knowledge is evident.[2]

Even a very young child may have an extraordinary, completely unaided and natural talent to add and subtract numbers but she is not as skillful in, for example, settling quarrels and avoiding them. It is easy to see the difference between, on the one hand, wisdom and virtue and, on the other hand, scientific knowledge and skills. A person can, at the same time, be highly intelligent but stupid, or even evil.

To give one enlightening yet gruesome example: If you visit the concentration camp at Dachau, just a few miles north of Munich, you can see an exhibition that portrays the methods of medical doctors before and during the Nazi

2. NE 1142a.

regime. The doctors used political prisoners and other enemies of the state to test how long humans can survive in
freezing water, and the method consisted of freezing people
to death in large vats. Of course, the data that they retrieved
was valid and even scientifically beneficial. The doctors
were not dumb but they were evil, and their high intelligence did not help them to avoid the moral horrors they
committed. Succeeding in that would have required virtues,
which they did not have to a sufficient degree.

Practical wisdom differs from all other virtues in that
it does not itself have a mean. You can never get too good
at finding the mean between the extremes; one cannot become too wise. Wisdom can grow without limit because
wisdom means the ability to apply rules and principles in
differing situations. Other virtues always involve right proportion. A generous person is not too generous (so that he
gives away all his belongings) but knows how to balance his
benevolence. Failing in generosity results from too narrow
a view. A person who is too generous is not temperate and
just. This is called the unity of virtues: succeeding in one
virtue is dependent on succeeding in others. Virtues cannot
be isolated from each other, and a practically wise person
is one who knows how to balance all the relevant virtues in
varying contexts.

VIRTUES IN DIFFERENT TRADITIONS

In ancient Greco-Roman philosophy, the four cardinal virtues were temperance, courage, justice, and wisdom. The
name "cardinal" comes from the Latin word for hinges (*car-
dines*); all the other virtues are dependent on these virtues as
hinges hold a door in its place. Drawing on 1 Cor 13:13, the
medieval Christian tradition adds three theological virtues
to these: faith, hope, and love. This is still perhaps the most

well-known way of listing virtues in our time. However, virtues are not something that only European or Christian philosophy recognizes. Other religions and philosophical traditions contain their own virtue theories and lists.

In Buddhism, the Noble Eightfold Path is one of the basic principles of ethical deliberation. To those who follow it, the path offers redemption from suffering through growth in wisdom. Central to this process is the concept of *samyañc*, which can be translated as right, complete, coherent, and whole. The virtues listed in the Path are: right view of life, right intention, right speech, right action, right livelihood, right effort, right mindfulness, and right concentration.

The Veda texts and Upanishads of Hinduism mention courage, forgiveness, temperance, freedom from lust, purity, deliberation, truthfulness, and freedom from anger as principal virtues. Other important ethical virtues are the principle of non-violence (*ahimsa*) and self-control, which are also underlined in Buddhist traditions.

Islam considers the prophet Muhammad as the incarnation of virtue and his pieces of advice (*hadith*) are the ground for ethical thought and conduct. Islamic theology has produced lists of virtues that are not that different from the traditions mentioned already. A special feature, however, is the emphasis on the virtue of obedience and fasting as the exercise that trains the person to live a life of self-control.

In the Old Testament, Proverbs contains several verses where virtues are presented through familiar images. For example, Proverbs 6:6 urges the reader, "Go to the ant, you sluggard; consider its ways and be wise!" The rabbinic tradition develops virtue theory so that peace and harmony (*shalom*) becomes the aim toward which Torah is directed.

Contemporary psychologists, especially those working in the tradition of so-called positive psychology, have been interested in virtues as they are understood in different cultures. Christopher Peterson and Martin Seligman argue that, even if there are differences in emphasis between cultures, the virtues fall nicely into six classes that can then be divided further into classes.[3] The list and taxonomy is not supposed to remain absolute but is more like a heuristic tool that helps us to get a grasp of virtues as a whole.

Wisdom and knowledge	Courage	Humanity
Creativity Love of learning Open-mindedness Perspective	Bravery Persistence Integrity Responsibility Vitality	Love Friendship Compassion Social Intelligence

Justice	Temperance	Transcendence
Loyalty Fairness Leadership	Forgiveness Humility Modesty Moderation Self-regulation	Appreciation of beauty Gratitude Hope Humor Faith Spirituality

It is customary to draw a distinction between moral and intellectual virtues. Intellectual virtues include, for example, open-mindedness, carefulness, honesty, intellectual courage, independence, and perseverance. However, it is not always possible to make a clear distinction between

3. Peterson and Seligman, *Character Strengths and Virtues*, 56

moral and intellectual virtues because some intellectual virtues require moral uprightness and vice versa.

HABITUATION AND VIRTUE

The ancient Greeks used the word "virtue" to denote all kinds of practical skills, like running and spear throwing. These skills were acquired through practice so that they were almost automatic and effortless. For example, a person who is a fast runner does not need to put in a lot of effort to run 100 meters in less than 15 seconds, whereas someone who has not practiced as much will be half dead after the run and with well over 20 seconds on the timer.

Soon the terminology starts to develop and become more precise, and skills and virtues are separated, while it is still held that both of these require practice and they can both become automatic and effortless. However, we do not consider a person who knows how to tie a bowtie virtuous; he is merely skillful. In order to pass as virtuous, one needs to have a larger set of both practical and theoretical character traits. Moreover, virtues require the ability to apply the knowledge in constantly changing environments in a coherent manner. It is not enough to know the rules of proper behavior but one needs to know how to employ them.

The practice of virtues is called habituation (from Latin *habitus*). *Habitus* is what enables a person to act in ways that are excellent. Sometimes *habitus* is called "the second nature," which underlines the automatic aspect of virtuous behavior. If someone possesses a virtuous habit, she will perform her actions effortlessly, immediately, and feels joy in doing so.

Virtuous action is related to a person's character through her temperament and acquired habits. Temperament means that part of your personality that is very hard to modify or change. For example, someone may be naturally gentle and therefore it is easy for her to be temperate and it is difficult to aggravate her, no matter how hard she is provoked. Acquired habits are easier to change. For example, let us think of a judge who has given verdicts in the past that he now, through greater experience and knowledge, considers to be unjust. This process of learning changes his habitus and remodels his actions so that he now makes just decisions. The first actual decision may be hard to make but making choices gets easier little by little.

According to traditional virtue theories, virtuous action can be brought about through four different routes. First, we can be naturally inclined toward certain virtuous behavioral patterns. Second, through repetition we can gain the ability to perform virtuous and moral actions. Third, we can practice rational deliberation so that we become disposed toward intellectual virtues. Fourth, in a theological context, we can perform actions that result from supernatural, infused virtues. These include the theological virtues of faith, hope, and love, which cannot be acquired through repetition and practice.

The process of virtuous habituation (there is also a vicious form of habituation, when one consistently chooses to do wrong) proceeds through the following stages:

a. We acknowledge the norm that tells us what is right and what is wrong.

b. We perform the right action.

c. Our actions become parts of our character so that we are more and more inclined toward the right and good.

d. Our understanding of the norms grows and we gain

the ability to apply these norms in new situations.[4]

As theory becomes practice, our character goes through changes and is formed into the image of the virtue, or vice. In the Aristotelian virtue tradition, theory and practice are intermingled; there cannot be one without the other. Virtue concerns our whole person, our intellect, will, and emotions. Based on this fundamental feature of virtue, C. S. Lewis makes an observation:

> Without the aid of trained emotions the intellect is powerless against the animal organism. I had sooner play cards against a man who was quite sceptical about ethics, but bred to believe that "a gentleman does not cheat," than against an irreproachable moral philosopher who had been brought up among sharpers. In battle it is not syllogisms that will keep the reluctant nerves and muscles to their post in the third hour of the bombardment. . . . And all the time—such is the tragi-comedy of our situation—we continue to clamour for those very qualities we are rendering impossible. You can hardly open a periodical without coming across the statement that what our civilization needs is more 'drive', or dynamism, or self-sacrifice, or 'creativity'. In a sort of ghastly simplicity, we remove the organ and demand the function. We make men without chests and expect of them virtue and enterprise. We laugh at honor and are shocked to find traitors in our midst. We castrate and bid the geldings be fruitful.[5]

Lewis' remark is meant as a criticism of a way of thinking that subscribes to the theory but forgets the means

4. Titus, "Moral Development and Connecting the Virtues."

5. Lewis, *Abolition of Man*, 26.

by which one is supposed to turn the theory into practice. The other, equally bad, extreme is to underline the practice without exercising judgment regarding the aims and means of the practice.

TRADITIONAL VIRTUE THEORY AND ITS CONTEMPORARY CHALLENGES

Traditional virtue theory contains three separate claims that define the nature of virtue: the Robustness Claim, the Stability Claim and the Interconnection, or Unity, Claim.[6] According to the Robustness Claim a virtuous person should always exhibit the same virtue, even if the context varies. For example, a soldier who is courageous on the battlefield should also be able to act courageously in mundane situations, and an honest person does not lie to people, regardless of whether he is speaking to his spouse, friends, or employer.

The Stability Claim means that virtues are acquired and deep-rooted character traits that cannot be altered easily and without considerable effort. An abstemious person will not turn into a drunkard overnight and a dishonest car salesperson will not suddenly stop cheating his or her customers. The Stability Claim does not mean that there will be no changes whatsoever, only that the changes will always take time and energy. Both virtues and vices can be acquired but it always takes practice.

According to the Interconnection Claim, virtues form a whole. The stronger version of this claim insists that all virtues are essentially one and the same. (Plato is sometimes presented as holding this view.) The weaker version claims only that virtues are supported by each other. Thus it is possible for a person to have a set of both virtues and

6. Timpe and Boyd, "Introduction," 7–9.

vices. The vices do not nullify the virtues but they prevent and hinder fully virtuous action, such as when, in a moment of intemperance, the person makes a bad, perhaps unjust, judgment.

The most well-known criticism of virtue theory is *situationism*, which challenges the aforementioned claims by drawing on empirical research that seems to undermine the existence of stable and action-guiding character traits.[7] If there are no traits, there cannot be any virtues either. The studies cited most often are the following:

- Hugh Hartshorne and Mark A. May's work, where they tested the honesty of school children, or more precisely, their propensity to lie, steal, and cheat in exams.

- Daniel Batson's "Good Samaritan" test, where he examined the eagerness of Princeton Theological Seminary students to help an unknown, sick man.

- Stanley Milgram's authority test, where the test subject was asked to give electric shocks to a patient (who was an actor).[8]

Based on these and other similar experiments, the critics have claimed that we do not possess the kind of virtuous character traits that the classical theory presupposes. Hartshorne and May's experiment demonstrated that the children did not have much in the way of cross-contextual patterns of behavior. For example, they could be honest to their classmates while being dishonest to their parents, or they could resist the temptation to steal but they could lie to help out their friends.

7. See, e.g., Doris, *Lack of Character*; Harman, "Moral Philosophy Meets Social Psychology"

8. Hartshorne and May, *Studies in the Nature of Character*; Batson, *Altruism Question*; Milgram, "Behavioral Study of Obedience."

Batson's test showed that external factors, like being in a hurry, predicted a person's behavior more than their supposed character traits. In the test, the subjects were asked to go from a lecture (where one group of subjects had heard a lecture on the Good Samaritan parable) to another building. On the way, there was a sick man lying on the ground. The first group was told that they were already late, the second that they should hurry so that they would not be late, and the third group was free to walk at their own pace. Only 10% of the first group helped the man, while 45% of the second group and 63% of the third group helped him. Attendance at the lecture and self-reported religiosity did not have a notable effect.

However, critics of situationism have pointed out how the experiments do not in fact prove all the things that they are presumed to prove.[9] They tell us something valuable about how people behave in certain contexts but they cannot be used to support strong situationist claims. I mention here only a few of the problems that prevent this argumentative move.

First of all, it is often very hard to tell exactly what "environment" and "context" mean, and there is no consensus even among the theorists themselves on the meaning and use of these terms. Therefore, controlling the effect of the environment becomes problematic, to say the least. Moreover, the context (broadly understood) includes the person's understanding and interpretation of the situation in which she takes herself to be. The "context" is thus not only outside the person but already inside the test subject. This blends the outside contextual factors and the individual's own interpretations so that we cannot really know what causes the

9. Thus, e.g., Hogan, "Much Ado about Nothing," 249; Jost and Jost, "Virtue Ethics and the Social Psychology of Character," 253–54; and Miller, *Character and Moral Psychology*, 85–107.

behavior and why. Often the reasons are not even transparent to the subjects themselves. Besides, the test subjects and those who construct the experiments may have different understandings of what is actually happening.

The second problem is the temporal narrowness of the experiments. In order to evaluate the traits of a person, we need to have data on his actions from different contexts and over a longer period of time. We cannot infer from the fact that John did X at moment t that John generally does X. Situationists typically accuse virtue theorists of an attribution error: when a person performs well, this is attributed to her character trait. However, the situationist can fall prey to an inverted attribution error: when a person performs badly, this is attributed to the context and environment.

Thirdly, the definition of a given virtue, and the manner of its proper application, is not necessarily clear. For example, is it right to put into your pocket a dollar you found or are you obliged to find its owner? If I think that "finders keepers" is a legitimate rule in some context, I will think that I am not breaking any rule if I keep the bill.

In the Milgram experiments the test subject is in a dissonant situation where one set of virtues (such as punctuality, loyalty to authorities, willingness to advance science) is in tension with compassion. The students had to perform a similar balancing act in the case of the Good Samaritan test. Furthermore, it is customary for us to evaluate the situation, such as the one confronted by the students, so that we think that the person is not in need of immediate assistance or that there are other people who can help them better. A person who has passed out is not necessarily a strong enough impulse to trigger the act of helping.

In the original Milgram test, almost all the subjects gave a lethal electric shock (to the actor) when they were pressured to do so by the scientist. In our culture, people have high respect for scientists (just as people in the past trusted priests and ministers), and they have a tendency to trust that they know what they are doing and that no one will really be harmed (of course, this is often an unwarranted belief). When the test was replicated so that there were two scientists supervising the test who disagreed whether dangerous shocks should be given, the test subjects stopped immediately. The spell of loyalty was broken and there was no tension between virtues, so compassionate action was enabled.

DO WE HAVE CHARACTER?

Even if situationism cannot disprove classical virtue theory, it does call it into question. The central issue debated in virtue theories is the existence of character, which is the seat of virtues in the human soul. The debate is complicated and I will only present some general features of it.

Among others, John Doris has suggested that virtue is limited such that it is possible for a person to be loyal to his friends but not to his wife.[10] As an absolute principle, however, this does not seem convincing. In the Aristotelian tradition, virtue is seen expressly as an ability. If Matthew is a good guitarist, he has both agile fingers and a sense of rhythm. When Matthew practices the guitar these are not two different skills but part of the same skill. Of course, it is possible for Matthew to be a natural beat machine but, at the same time, be all thumbs. In that case he would not be a good guitarist. Similarly, the fact that a person displays loyalty in some situations better than in others does not allow us to make judgments regarding the existence of character traits; instead we can only say that his loyalty is deficient.

10. Doris, *Lack of Character*.

In fact, current research shows that we do not have virtues or vices in the way they are typically understood in popular discourse, that is, as simple and rather static qualities of the soul. The popular view of virtues or vices is affected by paradigmatic examples like Mother Teresa or Hitler. But very few of us are like those exemplars, and even they were not totally good or evil. If we look at normal people, you and me, how do we behave, exactly? Obviously, we are not dramatically good or evil but exhibit a mixture of both virtues and vices in our actions. If someone were to look at our actions from a distance and only momentarily, she might get the idea that we are not very coherent in our actions. In one situation we do X, but soon we do Y, even if the situation looks more or less the same. So do the situationists have a case, after all?

Christian Miller has proposed a theory of *Mixed Character Traits* that takes into account the situationist critique while defending the central claims of traditional virtue theory.[11] Miller argues that we can possess a trait that enables us to act relatively consistently across different contexts. Despite this stability we are affected by several factors that change our behavior. These include things like:

a. Background influences in a situation: when action X is possible, there are factors that either prevent or encourage action X.

b. Activation of the moral norms and moral sentiments a person recognizes.

c. Conscious reasons to abide by recognized moral norms.

d. Alternative courses of action, such as the option of leaving X undone or the assumption that someone

11. Miller, *Character and Moral Psychology*; *Moral Character*.

else will do X.

e. Activation of a mixed character trait: an estimation of the relation between action X and moral principles.[12]

Miller's theory allows one to acknowledge that a person's choices can be both fragmentary and coherent. For example, a person can act in two separate, closely related situations in differing ways but the difference can be explained by other factors that can affect a person's choices.

Let us think about the following example. Three people, Jane, Joy, and Jean, are walking through Central Park. On their way, they see a man lying on the ground. Jane stops and helps the man, but Joy and Jean go past him. Joy has just received a message from her friend who has told her that she is considering committing suicide. Jean, seeing the man, spots also a park guard and she thinks that the guard can help the man more than she can. Jean is also small and she has recently been assaulted by a drunkard so she is afraid to approach the man. Jane, Joy, and Jean all share b and c but they differ in factors a, d, and e. Based on these differences, we cannot really say that these three people are morally different, or that Joy and Jean are less moral than Jane.

Miller argues that humans do not act like machines; our action patterns change all the time. Nevertheless, our actions do not fluctuate widely between the extremes but are relatively predictable. In fact, classical virtue theory does not presuppose that most people are able to act in a near-perfect manner. Instead, virtue is an ideal, toward which we are called to strive. Virtue theory requires only that virtues are possible, not that they are usual.

12. Miller, *Character and Moral Psychology*, 24–57.

THE UNITY OF VIRTUES

At first glance the idea that there is a unity or interconnection between virtues might sound strange. It is easy to come up with examples of people who display great strength of character and virtue in some matters but who fall considerably short in others. For example, Martin Luther King Jr. is known as a defender of civil rights beyond comparison, but he was repeatedly unfaithful to his wife. Oscar Schindler, who is known for helping Jews during World War II, was also an adulterer, an alcoholic, a gambler, and suffered from many negative character traits such as vanity. How should we think about these kinds of saints who failed? Are their laudable actions in the end only smoothed out vices or are these persons, according to virtue theory, worthy of esteem? The Unity Claim appears to prevent King and Schindler from being given the esteem that is due to them. A cynical assessment of these gentlemen would be that their upright behavior was only superficial and they were not genuinely good people.

Of all virtue theorists, Thomas Aquinas's precise conceptual distinctions make possible a careful handling of this question.[13] According to Thomas, it is possible for people to increase in virtue but at the same time fail to achieve this goal in several different ways. So what factors cause a well-intentioned person to fail frequently?

First, every one of us has a unique personal history and set of cognitive skills. We react to different stimuli in different ways: one person is more disposed than another to intervene in injustices, depending on background and experience. Even such mundane matters as the size of our body can have an influence. A well-built bodybuilder may be more ready to defend someone being bullied than

13. Titus, "Moral Development and Connecting the Virtues."

someone who is by nature slender and shy. A poor person is less able to be generous than a rich person. (Although it does not follow that a rich person who donates money to charities is being genuinely generous; the poor person may be, in truth, more generous but is just not in a position to give as much as someone who is rich.)

Second, we may have habits that are rooted so deeply in us that freeing ourselves from them can take a long time. In this case a person may continue to do the bad things that he is used to doing. Freedom from such habits comes only by learning other, better ways. Progress nevertheless comes slowly and in stages.

Third, it is entirely possible that someone who generally acts rightly can do something grossly wrong. There can be various reasons for this, such as tiredness, a lack of information, or an incorrect judgment. According to Aquinas, an isolated wrong action does not, however, lead to loss of a virtue because the virtue has, with practice, become a permanent character trait. A person can thus fail with regard to a particular act while his virtuous attitude is preserved.

Fourth, the presence of all virtues is, in the end, a matter of degree. For this reason, every person has a unique profile of virtues. One person has more patience than another. One person has more of a tendency to drink too much than another. In practice what this means is that, despite someone having the right disposition about something, his emotions and will can be weak and it is difficult for him not to act wrongly, or acting rightly requires a lot of effort. Nevertheless, if that person's disposition toward the matter remains intact, it is a case of momentary vice. Even this is serious, of course, because it can lead to bad habits which are no longer considered bad.

In Aquinas' view, King's actions were commendable and even worthy of praise. Despite this, his actions were nevertheless deficient because virtues did not completely guide his behavior. It is possible to understand the unity of virtues such that a particular vice prevents me from being as virtuous as I could be. For example, if I am usually generous but at the same time cynical, this can prevent me from being of help in situations where there is a need for generosity. In this way, virtues really are dependent on each other. The writer G. K. Chesterton devotes attention to the fact that many known examples of vices are actually deficient forms of virtue:

> The modern world is not evil; in some ways the modern world is far too good. It is full of wild and wasted virtues. When a religious scheme is shattered (as Christianity was shattered at the Reformation), it is not merely the vices that are let loose. The vices are, indeed, let loose, and they wander and do damage. But the virtues are let loose also; and the virtues wander more wildly, and the virtues do more terrible damage. The modern world is full of the old Christian virtues gone mad. The virtues have gone mad because they have been isolated from each other and are wandering alone. Thus some scientists care for truth; and their truth is pitiless. Thus some humanitarians only care for pity; and their pity (I am sorry to say) is often untruthful. For example, Mr. Blatchford attacks Christianity because he is mad on one Christian virtue: the merely mystical and almost irrational virtue of charity. He has a strange idea that he will make it easier to forgive sins by saying that there are no sins to forgive. Mr. Blatchford is not only an early Christian, he is the only early Christian who ought really to have been eaten by lions. For in his case the pagan accusation is really true: his mercy would mean mere anarchy. He really

is the enemy of the human race—because he is so human. As the other extreme, we may take the acrid realist, who has deliberately killed in himself all human pleasure in happy tales or in the healing of the heart. Torquemada tortured people physically for the sake of moral truth. Zola tortured people morally for the sake of physical truth. But in Torquemada's time there was at least a system that could to some extent make righteousness and peace kiss each other. Now they do not even bow. But a much stronger case than these two of truth and pity can be found in the remarkable case of the dislocation of humility.[14]

Aquinas says the same as Chesterton by declaring that a blind horse can certainly run fast, but the faster it runs, the worse it hurts itself and others. Evil comes about when something good is aimed for to the neglect of other good things. A particular virtue is a vice when it is raised above others. It is quite easy to present oneself as virtuous by emphasising a single good thing that is not balanced against other goods (populist politicians and do-gooders often fall into this). It is a lot more difficult to recognise many good things and try to balance them together. This is what the unity of virtues requires.

DO YOU NEED TO SUCCEED IN BEING VIRTUOUS?

According to Aristotle, in order for a person to be virtuous, it is essential that she succeed in achieving the intended good state of affairs with her actions and choices. The Stoics, however, thought that this is not absolutely necessary

14. Chesterton, *Orthodoxy*, 27.

even though it is desirable. The demand according to Aristotle's definition is called the success component. According to Julia Annas, virtues can be examined in two ways.[15] First, the virtuous person's acts should have the right *telos*, or final goal. This refers to a complete attitude toward life which reflects the greatest possible number of virtues. On the other hand, a virtuous person's acts always have *skopos* or an immediate target, a certain good at which he aims: that kitten I want to save, this feeling of pride I want to suppress, or that foolhardy stunt I leave undone.

It feels natural to assume that, to be virtuous, it is enough for a person to have a virtuous *telos*. *Skopos* is a desirable addition but not to be demanded absolutely. Let us imagine a parallel universe in which there is a different ending to the movie *Saving Private Ryan*. In this alternative scenario, Ryan is already dead when the search party reaches him. In order to reach him they have had to carry out many heroic acts. By Aristotle's strict definition, the rescuers would not be virtuous. Or think about it from the point of view of intellectual virtues. It is natural for us to think that individuals such as Ptolemy, Galileo, Newton, and Einstein are good examples of many intellectual virtues. However, between them, their beliefs are very different. Einstein's beliefs about the nature of the universe are more precise and realistic than Ptolemy's. But must we then think that Ptolemy is less virtuous than Newton? This feels like an exaggeration.

Let us think about another situation. A person who is known for his short-temper and who constantly explodes at people around him becomes contrite and starts to regret his behavior. However, a change in his behavior does not come about easily. He will lose his temper just as easily as before, regardless of not wanting it to happen. Is this person

15. Annas, "The Structure of Virtue," 15–33.

virtuous? This question takes us to a new level of complexity. The person in question clearly does not display the virtue of patience, but his situation is nevertheless better than before. That being the case, it is most natural to answer the question of the necessity of success on a case-by-case basis. In some cases the success component is necessary and in others it clouds the virtue of the actions.

CAN VIRTUES BE LEARNED?

Philosophers have traditionally thought that virtues can certainly be taught, but there have been disagreements about how this can best be done and how difficult it is. Naturally, key questions have also been what virtues to teach and how to interpret them. But is there any evidence, apart from our own intuition (or lack of it), that one can develop in virtues? In our own time, positive psychology has started to investigate this question. We will look at positive psychology more closely in chapter 4, but for now we will refer just to those results that relate to learning the virtues.

How much do we know? A key positive psychology volume goes through all the evidence (available at that time) and deems it to be rather deficient.[16] Another wide-ranging, more interdisciplinary handbook by Kevin Timpe and Craig Boyd does not contain much new empirical material that would strengthen the empirical basis of theories of virtue or positive psychology to any significant extent. The book's emphasis is on the different kinds of capacities in human nature that make learning virtues possible in principle.[17] For example, both of these books consider the natural human ability to mimic behavior in their environment, which certainly provides a good basis for learning

16. Peterson and Seligman, *Character Strengths and Virtues*.
17. Timpe and Boyd, *Virtues and Their Vices*.

both virtues and vices. Nevertheless, although there are signs that virtue improves wellbeing and that some virtues can possibly be cultivated, our knowledge of human nature in this respect is very fragmentary. Despite there having been no vigorous empirical investigation of virtues for very long, recent research does seem to confirm the idea that learning virtues is indeed possible although not especially easy.

There are significant problems regarding learning virtues. At one stage it was thought, rather naïvely from today's perspective, that all education required was mechanical repetition of rote-learned mantras, wallcharts, and the upkeep of positive, authoritative examples, but this has turned out to be a clearly deficient strategy. The reason for this is that external, mechanical participation does not necessarily influence a person deeply. According to positive psychology, the foundation for action needs to be internalized moral virtue. In Aristotle's view, in order for an act to be a virtue, it must fulfil the following conditions:

a. the act must be moral;

b. the act must be done for right reasons and motives;

c. the act must be done as a good in itself, not only as a means to an end.

Aristotle holds that, if we start to train people just to act rightly, we have a problem. An act that is in itself right but which is done from wrong motives can justifiably be considered a vice. A politician, for example, who pushes through some reforms so that he will be re-elected is not a very moral politician (although he may be a good populist).

According to Kristján Kristjánsson, who has studied the philosophy and psychology of virtues, a consequence of this is both a psychological and a moral paradox.[18] The psy-

18. Kristjánsson, *Virtues and Vices*, 202–5.

chological paradox relates to teaching a person something, and the associated emotions. If as a child you went to piano lessons or you played football, you may end up with a life-long love of those pursuits—or you may hate them from the bottom of your heart. If virtues are learned by practicing them, how can we ensure that the person starts to love a virtue rather than hating it?

The moral paradox relates to the role of authority. In virtue theory it is often required that the older educator knows what the good is that he imparts to the younger learners. If, however, a requirement of virtue is that the learner knows how to strive for what is good, does this contradict the fact that the form of the good has to be taught to her?

No simple solution to these paradoxes exists. One way to address them is to state that teaching virtues in itself requires a way of thinking and acting that corresponds with the idea of the unity of virtues. For this reason, teaching virtues is just as hard as practising them. Virtues cannot be learned mechanically or by rote. Rather, they require internalized wisdom, and not even this guarantees that the lesson will be learned. Virtue is frail.

QUESTIONS FOR CONSIDERATION

1. Define "virtue" and "vice".

2. Do you need to succeed in being virtuous in order to be truly virtuous?

3. What is meant by the unity of virtues? Give an example.

4. What kind of criticisms are there against virtue theorization? How would you respond to them?

2

THE HISTORY OF VIRTUES

AN INTERESTING AND LIVELY discussion about virtues is going on—in fact it has been going on for over 2000 years. The first thinkers in history defined virtuousness as a central principle of a life fully lived. However, there are many nuances connected with virtues and at different times virtuousness has been defined in somewhat divergent ways. In this chapter we will consider how virtue theory started to develop in ancient Greece, how Christianity influenced its interpretation and how, since the Enlightenment, a considerable range of virtues have been known about.

THE VIRTUES OF A HEROIC SOCIETY

The phrase "heroic society" typically refers to the stage in human history when stories of heroes had a central role.[1] It is mainly a term from literary studies that has been applied in historical research. Key works of the heroic period

---

1. Virtues of heroic societies are discussed in MacIntyre, *After Virtue*.

in Western culture include, among others, Homer's *Iliad* and *Odyssey*, the Germanic *Song of the Nibelungs*, the Saxon *Beowulf*, and the Finnish *Kalevala*. In the case of ancient Greece, the period of heroic society was in the time before the birth of Greek democracy, and in northern Europe it extended until Christianization and even continued long after that. In the Far East, heroic culture has survived longer than in the West and has become familiar to westerners via film and literature.

In heroic societies, virtue is fundamentally connected with social roles. People have, by birth, a certain role that they have to stay faithful to and they must carry out the associated responsibilities. As well as the individual person, there are also clear social structures such as relations, family, and fatherland. For example, in Confucianism virtue is defined through various relationships, with precise stipulations on the responsibilities of both parties. There are five basic relationships: between governor and governed, between parent and child, between a husband and his wife, between an older and a younger brother, and between friends. If, for one reason or another, the responsibilities are not met, the result is shame. Making amends for an offence like this can often be very tragic.

For example, in *47 Ronin*, a famous Japanese tale based on a true event, the samurais take revenge for the death of their leader. Due to the fact that both the leader's death (he committed *seppuku* after having injured the court official who had insulted him) and the actual revenge (the samurais defied the shogun's prohibition of seeking revenge for their leader's fate) are morally difficult cases, the whole act of revenge is problematic in relation to the code of honor. The story ends with the samurai regaining their honor, but they nevertheless have to kill themselves to preserve their honor and break the cycle of violence.

In Homer's *Iliad* the word for virtue refers to any excellent skill or ability, such as the ability to run quickly, to fight well, to be witty, and even the ability to trick enemies. Accordingly, treachery and lying could be virtues, and suffering defeat, being forced to adopt a lower status, and having to submit to somebody else's rule were vices. This underlines the fact that heroic societies' concept of virtue is localized: virtues serve a certain, quite small social circle, relatives and family, and they are accorded absolute value. From our perspective, it is difficult to appreciate the reason for the Trojan War. The Trojan prince, the handsome Paris, kidnaps the Spartan king Menelaus' wife and takes her to Troy. Menelaus gathers a great army and sets off to get his wife back. The war lasts nine years and a huge number of people are killed, all because Menelaus' honor has been insulted. Virtue demands a return of the honor despite a very heavy price.

In heroic societies, virtues and societal life are intimately connected. Alasdair MacIntyre explains:

> Any adequate account of the virtues in heroic society would be impossible which divorced them from their context in its social structure, just as no adequate account of the social structure of heroic society would be possible which did not include an account of the heroic virtues. But to put it in this way is to understate the crucial point: morality and social structure are in fact one and the same in heroic society.[2]

The central material of Greek tragedy comes from these roots. The Greek tragedies often focused on the dilemma that arises from the faithfulness of two different people to their own virtues. Usually they result in a stalemate that is solved by some god who dictates from on high

2. MacIntyre, *After Virtue*, 123.

each one's place. The expression *deus ex machina* (literally "god from the machine") comes from this: god descends onto the stage with the help of a winch at the end of the play. This expression is used nowadays to refer to a surprising plot resolution in which an entirely new character is introduced, with whose help an apparently unresolvable situation is resolved.

The Greek plays portray a change that gradually happened in heroic societies. Thinking had already been taken in this direction by the pre-Socratic philosophers, such as Heraclitus and Xenophanes, who showed how the concept of the good appears to rest on arbitrary customs. In the new way of thinking, it is no longer only virtues at the level of the family that are important but virtues at a higher level: that of the *polis*, or city-state. The resolution of interpersonal conflicts arising from virtues moves beyond one's immediate sphere to the democratic decision-making body.

PLATO

Plato's dialogues are quite different to heroic stories in the way they relate to virtues. In many of his dialogues Plato steers the participants' rather heroic-sounding ideas onto a crash course with each other and, in this way, attempts to show that genuine virtue is something greater and better than what immediately comes to anyone's mind. Presenting Plato's teaching on virtues systematically is, however, far from simple. He approaches the matter in different ways in different works and his teaching on virtue goes through a certain amount of development from his earliest to his latest works. Plato does, however, commit to a eudaimonistic (Gr. *eu*, good, *daimon*, spirit) principle: a person naturally aims for happiness, and virtues are an essential way of achieving it.

The earliest dialogues touch upon definitions of the various virtues, and the aim is mostly negative: Plato shows how conventional definitions are deficient. In *Phaedo*, Plato emphasizes the corrupting influences of the world and guides the reader from the attractions of the sensual world toward asceticism. In *Protagoras*, Plato sketches out the concept of the unity of virtues, by which it is possible to create a more complete picture of what true happiness (*eudaimonia*) in a positive sense should involve.

In *Euthyphro*, Plato starts to develop his Theory of Forms. He reasons that, if we are to strive for the good, and if there are many good things, they must have a common denominator (which Plato calls *ideas* or *paradeigma*). However, these common denominators are, by nature, quite abstract, such as beauty and justice, and understanding them is not easy. In other words, understanding the idea of justice requires a particular kind of reflection that is not possible for everyone. Justice or the other ideas cannot, however, be merely human creations but must really exist independent of the human mind—otherwise we would have just gone back to heroic and relativistic thinking. The consequence of this is Platonic dualism: this physical world reflects only imperfectly the world of the Forms.

In *The Republic*, Plato presents a broad theory about society and the individual person's correct place. The conversation gets going with Thrasymachus' claim that the rule of the strongest is, in the end, the best measure of justice: "might makes right!" (Thrasymachus speaks partly with the voice of the heroic world but also with the voice of democracy, which Plato detests.) Plato takes a completely different approach to building his ideal state:

> The origin of the city, then, in my opinion, is to be found in the fact that we do not severally suffice for our own needs, but each of us lacks many

> things. . . .As a result of this, one man calling in
> another for one service and another for another,
> we, being in need of many things, gather many
> into one place of abode as associates and help-
> ers, and to this dwelling together we give the
> name city or state, do we not?[3]

In order for people's different needs to be met, we
need ways of preventing the system from collapsing. In
Plato's opinion, states have only poorly succeeded in pro-
ducing virtuous people, so the parameters of his ideal state
are quite precise. In ancient Greece it was typical to think
that a person receives, by birth, a particular status. Society
is therefore naturally divided into workers, soldiers, and
philosophers. According to Plato these match an individual's mental faculties. He holds that the soul is composed
of three parts: reason, will, and desire. Respectively, philosophers have reason, soldiers display will, and workers
express desire. Each class has its own typical virtues: wisdom (*sofia*), courage (*andreia*), and prudence (*sofrosyne*).
In addition, justice (*dikaiosyne*) is listed in *The Republic*
as a fourth virtue. In *Laws* a fifth virtue, piety (*hosiotes*),
joins the list. Thus Plato has presented both the ideal way
in which an individual should act and a picture of the ideal
state.

Plato describes in *The Republic* exactly how each class
can develop itself in regard to its typical virtues. Soldiers
should engage in a suitable amount of sport. Philosophers
may not own possessions or have a family and they should
devote their whole life to the practice of philosophy. During a philosopher's lifelong training there are unpleasant
periods of governing that nevertheless develop the philosopher's character. Plato's teaching on virtue focuses mainly
on philosophers since the philosophical way of life is seen

3. Republic II369b-c.

as the most valuable of all. A virtuous philosopher develops himself constantly; a good person is a good thinker. It is a little surprising that no exercises in particular are prescribed for the working class, but they may enjoy life and the works of their hands as long as they acknowledge their subservience.

Plato's ideal state has received a lot of criticism. Is his state really one in which happiness is maximized? Plato's system is openly aristocratic, undemocratic, and does not allow deviation. It is perhaps not surprising that the book has been an encouragement to various totalitarian utopias. The problems of Platonic utopia have often been depicted in movies (see for example *Man of Steel* and *Snowpiercer*).

It must be remembered, however, that the context in which Plato wrote was not Western democracy but rather a time of transition out of destructive tribal wars. At that time the city-states existed with the constant threat of complete collapse. On the other hand, Plato's model can be seen as a certain compromise in which everyone has to give up something in order for everybody to gain something that they consider good. Later, Plato defines the parameters of a good life and those of the state slightly differently: the state of *The Republic* is consciously utopian, while *Laws* defines the second-best option. In actual fact, there are rather few virtuous people and not even the best (not even philosophical) training prevents a person from becoming a wrongdoer. Therefore, a state does well to depend more on laws, commonly agreed upon rules, which should nevertheless reflect the idea of the Good. Emotions are no longer seen unambiguously as only interferences, but virtue is defined as the balance between reason and emotion. This definition prepares the way for Aristotle's virtue theory.

ARISTOTLE

The starting point for Aristotle's virtue theory is the concept of *eudaimonia*, which can be translated with the words such as "happiness", "flourishing", or "complete wellbeing" (Gr. *eu zeen*, living well).[4] Virtues, which are characteristics that make living well possible, are needed in order to realize happiness. According to Aristotle, "[*eudaimonia*] is the activity of the soul according to virtue."[5] Happiness is a value and a goal in itself; nobody wants to achieve happiness merely en route to another goal. Likewise, many good things, such as property or honor, do not contain happiness although they can assist in bringing it about. Happiness is something that is realized in different ways in different matters; it can be described as the full realization of what something is. In Aristotelian philosophy this is described with the word *telos*, goal. The goal of a knife is to cut sharply; a tree's goal is to grow tall and bear fruit; a pig's goal is to lie in the mud, and so on. All these goals are defined according to the nature of the matter at hand. But how then should a human person's *telos* be defined?

In order to understand Aristotle's concept of virtue, we first need to say something about his concept of a person, which he presents especially in his work *Nicomachean Ethics*. According to Aristotle the human soul is divided into irrational and rational parts which are each further divided into two. The irrational part of the soul consists of the vegetative soul and the animal soul. The vegetative soul is the connector between a person and the living world and it is passive in character. The animal soul connects a person

4. In the following sections I have used Jennifer Herdt's *Putting on Virtue*, which is an extensive historical treatment of virtues and strongly recommended for anyone interested in the historical development of Aristotelian virtue theory.

5. NE 1099b.

to the animal kingdom and its key characteristics are the abilities to sense, move, and desire various things. The desire of the animal soul is nevertheless irrational in the sense that animals do not have the ability to consider things at a higher level, which would enable reflection on various desires and evaluation of them. In people, however, a rational part to the soul, the ability to consider by dint of reason, is mingled with the irrational part. The two components of the rational part of the soul are scientific judgement together with contemplation (*sophia*) and practical reason (*phronesis*). *Sophia* concerns how things really are, whereas *phronesis* relates to action, namely, what I should do in each situation. According to Aristotle, a good person is someone in whom the irrational and rational parts work together in such a way as to express the good typical of a person. In this way, a person's *telos* is to be virtuous.

Aristotle also refers to virtue with the concept of *hexis*, the later Latin equivalent of which is typically *habitus*. *Hexis* does not, however, refer to a way that is passive and unknowing or to a custom (as can the English word "habit"). Rather, Aristotle thinks that virtue is an active state that requires us to work for it. According to Aristotle, regarding a virtuous person, "first he must act with knowledge; secondly he must deliberately choose the act, and choose it for its own sake; and thirdly the act must spring from a fixed and permanent disposition of character."[6] In other words, it is not enough that we just do externally right deeds, but a virtuous person should have a right attitude. In order for an act to be right, it has to combine "right reason" and "right will."[7]

The idea of virtue as the middle way between extremes also comes from Aristotle. What is in question here is not

6. NE 1105a.
7. NE 1139a, 24–6.

a mathematical centerpoint, nor was Aristotle referring to some kind of tame average or compromise. Rather, the middle way means the right quantity in each situation. Aristotle gives as an example the wrestler Milo who eats a meal of ten eggs, when two would suffice for a normal person. Correspondingly, in one situation there is no basis for getting angry while in another there is. In this way action that appears extreme may actually be the middle way in a particular situation. Connected with finding the middle way is the fact that there are many different layers in an action, none of which can be evaluated in the same way. We can imagine the following situation, for example. I unwrap a chocolate bar in my office, and I am preparing to eat it all myself. But, just then, my colleague walks in, and I decide to share the bar of chocolate with her. Just as we have shared out the pieces, a third colleague comes in, and we each give him about 17 percent of our portions. The chocolate is certainly mathematically divided between us, but now, while decreasing my quantity of chocolate, I increase my and my colleague's happiness in a way that cannot be fitted into an abstract formula.

One way that virtue and vice are distinct from each other is that no middle way can be defined for a vice, because something bad is always wrong. For example, if someone commits adultery, it does not make it less tragic that he committed it with a particular person at a particular time and in a particular place. Therefore, it is as if there are two sides to Aristotle's virtue ethics. On the one hand, ethics cannot be fitted into a formula (because the middle way varies according to the situation), but on the other hand, some acts are always wrong irrespective of the situation (because they are bad by nature).

Aristotle compares a good deed and a virtue to a sculpture that is done skillfully: it has the right proportions, it is harmonious, and it pleases the observer. Therefore, to him it is natural to describe an object of virtue as beautiful (*kalon*). For Aristotle, virtues are expressly beautiful and therefore worth pursuing in themselves. Aristotle makes a distinction between a noble (*kalos kai agathos*) person and a good (*agathos*) person. If both of them were asked why they helped a first-grader to cross a busy junction, their answers would be similar: so that cars would not hit the child. However, if the question is revised so as to ask why one should prevent cars from hitting a child in the first place or why one should act virtuously, their answers start to differ. A person who is only good will not necessarily be able to answer the question at all, or he will state how virtue benefits the subject in different ways. A noble person, however, will answer by referring to the virtue of the act in itself; he does good for its own sake.

Like Plato, Aristotle also thinks that guidance toward the good must start while a person is young, when the environment plays a large role. The educator's job is to guide the young person onto the right road, which happens via a process of habituation in which the young person learns to recognise what is good and what is bad. In our first chapter we saw how certain paradoxes are associated with the idea of habituation, and Aristotle was aware of them. At the center of the theory of virtue that Aristotle presents is a certain chicken or egg problem regarding precedence. One becomes virtuous by doing virtuous acts: "It is correct therefore to say that a man becomes just by doing just actions and temperate by doing temperate actions; and no one can have the remotest chance of becoming good without doing them."[8] Aristotle nevertheless notes how this teaching contains a particular contradiction: "For if they do just and temperate actions, they are just and temperate already, just

8. NE 1105b.

as, if they spell correctly or play in tune, they are scholars or musicians."[9] In other words, I need to do good in order to become good, but in order to do good I need to be good already.

A learner can be motivated by an external or internal reward. Let us think of a child whose parents take her to piano lessons. The child does not especially like playing the piano, but she gets a reward every time she does her homework well and shows progress. This is external motivation, equivalent to the external good that comes from doing good. However, the parents' hope is that the child would learn to *enjoy* playing the piano, not because of rewards or fear of punishment but because of piano playing in itself. In the same way, a genuinely virtuous person does good not for a reward but because of the good in itself.

A later tradition gives attention to this problem by emphasizing the question of whether learning virtue involves pretending. In order to learn a virtue, a person has to pretend to be something other than he is. In current discussion this is called the habituation gap, a gap between the reality and the ideal. The existence of this gap is one factor that leads thinkers to adopt different ideas of the nature of virtue.

Aristotle's virtue theory therefore contains unresolved tensions. According to Aristotle a virtuous person can be described as having a quality called magnanimity (Gr. *megalopsykhia,* Lat. *magnanimitas*). A magnanimous person is able to appraise herself in just the right way. She does not underrate herself and her abilities, and neither is she proud or demanding of credit for things that are not of her doing. According to Aristotle, magnanimity is associated with an awareness of independence. However, this seems to be in contradiction with what Aristotle has previously said about

9. NE1105a.

how it is possible to become virtuous in the first place. Learning virtue requires a good upbringing, wise parents, a good circle of friends, and just laws. The Christian critique of Aristotle has, to a large extent, focused on integrating a revised concept of magnanimity with other virtues.

AUGUSTINE

Augustine, the Church Father, forms his own conception of virtues from within the tension between ancient Greek virtue theory and Christian theology. On the one hand, many statements of ancient Greek philosophers sound very reasonable to him but, on the other hand, something in them sounds wrong. The expression *splendida vitia*, splendid vices, is often associated with Augustine's conception of virtue, an expression with which he is said to have described pre-Christian teaching on virtue. In fact, Augustine never used that expression, although in part it correctly represents his ambivalent attitude to the classical inheritance.

In some ways Augustine praises Roman virtues effusively, going as far as to portray them as a model for Christians. For example, in *The City of God* (5, XVIII), Brutus is presented as having murdered his child for the benefit of Rome. Augustine asks why, if the pagan Brutus makes such a great sacrifice for earthly good, would Christians not also adopt this all-surrendering attitude—even when such extreme actions are not demanded of Christians?

In other ways, according to Augustine, even the best Roman virtue fails to reach the level of Christian virtue, and often what is a vice for Romans is a virtue for Christians, and vice versa. The reason for this is that the non-Christian is not able to form a right relationship with the object of his love. Even his best acts of love are somehow tainted. As an example, Augustine refers to the famous story of the suicide of Lucretia. In Roman history Lucretia was a noble maiden who was raped by Sextus, the son of the Etruscan king who ruled Rome. As a result, Lucretia killed herself with a dagger. Lucretia's suicide stirred up the anger of Romans and, in the end, led to them driving the Etruscan conquerors out. To the Romans, Lucretia was a model of the virtue of courage. Later, they also put her forward as a model for Christian women who had been raped by the barbarians. This is connected with the idea that someone who has been raped suffers great shame and can only be freed from it by death. Augustine opposes this interpretation, however. For him, suicide is never a virtue. It does not reflect the subject's level of virtue but rather her weakness.

In criticizing the Roman conceptions of virtue, Augustine builds on Aristotle's theory. According to Augustine, Aristotle's magnanimous and noble person is an incomplete answer to the question of why we should be virtuous. For example, the pursuit of honor for the sake of honor itself is, according to Augustine, a vice, because it makes a person's priorities wrong. Honor and thanks certainly do follow right actions, but they must not be the aim of the actions. To put it more precisely, Augustine claims that, in Roman virtue theory, one cannot love virtue in the right way but virtue is always a way of achieving some goal. Augustine does commit to the same eudaimonistic framework as Plato and Aristotle: a person always aims for happiness, and virtue is a way of reaching it. However, he differs from his predecessors in his account of what, ultimately, we can love as the goal in itself. First, virtue is, in this world, always imperfect and people's motives are always impure. Second, only God in his perfection can be a goal in himself. The key difference between Augustine and the Greek philosophers is their understanding of dependence and independence, not the idea of striving for happiness in itself.

Several critics have noted a central problem in Augustine's thinking.[10] According to him, things in the world can be divided into those that one should use (*uti*) and those that one enjoys (*frui*). Only God belongs in the latter category, and everything that is created belongs in the former. God should be loved as an end in himself, not used as a means toward another end. Does this mean that we should love people as a means of loving God more perfectly? Augustine denies us this option. He thinks that people's natural ability to love things is good in itself, but sin has corrupted us so that we are unable to love things rightly. Our feelings are not very good guides regarding the worth of the objects of our desires. According to Augustine, we can love virtues, our neighbors, and all other created things rightly only if they are understood as God's good gifts. It is important to understand that the value of created reality comes from God, who is the creator and giver of everything. This viewpoint makes it impossible to use works of love, for example, to please God and as a way of winning God's favor.

In Augustine's thinking, God changes, in a certain sense, the way that people by nature value different things. First, the move from unbelief to belief requires conversion, which changes a person's priorities. In addition, when someone progresses in their faith, the way they relate to things changes; those objects that the person at one time loved greatly lose their significance when they are replaced by better objects of love. For example, if someone previously derived great enjoyment from gladiator fights, now he delights in being able to help the poor.

An issue related to this is the worthiness of a virtue and a person's autonomy in Augustine's thinking. According to him, a person is unable to achieve the right frame

10. For an extensive treatment of this particular question, see Gregory, *Politics and the Order of Love*, 325–81.

of mind (which a perfect virtue requires) without God's help. In regard to this, it is possible to distinguish between enlightenment of the intellect (*illuminatio*) and a new desire of the will (*delectatio*). In this way a person first comes to know what is right and in addition wants to do what is right. When someone sees something perfectly beautiful he cannot fail to be enthralled. Presently, however, no one can see God unless God reveals himself. Therefore a person's virtue and love are radically dependent on God's action. The goal of Christian love is not independence, as was the case in Aristotle's idea of magnanimity. On the contrary, love connects the lover to what she loves, so that her freedom expands in union with her beloved.

Can a person influence their own level of virtue? This question is multifaceted. On the one hand, Augustine emphasizes human dependence on God's initiative, and, on the other hand, he underlines human responsibility for how we use our own will. In the view of non-Christian philosophers, Augustine appears to reject the idea of human responsibility. Worse still, if virtue is not a human characteristic, is it not pretense that we are dealing with here, or some kind of mask that, when worn by a Christian, turns him into something that in reality he is not? Augustine himself nevertheless recognizes this problem by referring to actors in the theater who play a role but are themselves quite different from the role they play. The answer to this problem is not to leave good works undone, because the final result would naturally be absurd: one could not do any good because there would always be the possibility that the deed would not be genuinely virtuous, but a vice. Rather, a person must do good, following the ideal that people better than him have given him.

Although Augustine thinks that truly good deeds are possible only for Christians, in the end this is only a theoretical possibility. Actually, the difference between a Christian and a pagan is not necessarily very big, because even a Christian lives in a world disfigured by evil that prevents perfect virtue from becoming visible—and evil is present in Christians, too. Even a Christian's efforts toward perfection are always partial and can reveal many kinds of weakness. Nevertheless, a Christian's job is to imitate Christ's example and obey his commands. Progress in this is a very slow process.

Virtue grows by imitation (*imitatio*). A negative example of imitation for Augustine is the theater, which, like Plato, he criticized. Plato's criticism concerned the inadequacy of the theater for correctly depicting reality, being something that depicts something that depicts something: in other words a play is one step further away from ideas than the reality that is manifest to us. In Augustine's view, the theater and gladiator fights present vices to us, but the key aspect of his critique regards how we relate to what we see. Not all art and theater is worthless, according to him. Every Christian has reason to know the contents of the classical plays, for example, because they are part of a general education. According to him, the popularity of traditional Greek plays had, however, recently declined and people were being shown more and more spectacles and gladiator fights, which had the purpose of stirring powerful emotions in the absence of powerful contents, and by enjoying watching this rubbish people were in danger of becoming like it. In his view bad theater weakens our empathy when faced with genuine suffering. In the theater we see things that would normally arouse in us the desire to help, but nobody is so silly as to react to something in the show as they would in real life. We don't give of ourselves to the actors in Hugo's *Les Miserables*, even though they have brought our feelings of empathy to the surface. Watching a play therefore links, in a bad way, the right and wrong reaction, in other words pity and passivity in the face of suffering. The best kind of theater, however, is the liturgy of the church: "Contrast that holy spectacle with the pleasures and delights of the theater. There your eyes are defiled, here your eyes are cleaned. Here the spectator deserves praise if he but imitate what he sees; there he is bad, and if he imitates what he sees he becomes infamous."[11]

The central theme of the classical philosophers was how virtue and happiness are connected with each other. It is clear that all people strive to maximize their happiness. But people, and philosophers, understand happiness in very different ways. For example, according to the Stoics, virtue is enough for happiness. No external good things are necessary because, if happiness depended on them, we would immediately become unhappy if they were taken away. Augustine also thinks that a correct theory of virtue must describe happiness as independent of external good things.

On the other hand, Augustine notes that perfect happiness is not possible in this life since we are under constant threat of some misfortune. The problem of classical virtue theory is that it places too high a responsibility on the individual. We cannot control our surroundings, and we cannot even fully control our own behavior. Consequently, happiness in this world is something that escapes us. This is often called Augustinian realism, and it has had a significant influence on later political philosophy. Yet it must be said that this is visible in Augustine's writing only as a general attitude; one cannot consider it his fully-defined political theory. According to Augustinian realism it is unwise to strive toward the kinds of goals that are practically impossible for

11. Quoted in Herdt, *Putting on Virtue*, 64. Migne, *Patrologia Latina* XLVI, 879

us to reach. This is a counterbalance to political idealism. Attempts to realize a society like the one in Plato's *Republic* would have caused Augustine to shake his head.

THOMAS AQUINAS

Of all medieval theologians, Thomas Aquinas in particular developed a detailed theory of virtue, and its influence has been immense.[12] As a result of Aquinas, there was renewed interest in Aristotle's virtue theory, and it became part of mainstream Christian theology. Aquinas set about giving pagan virtues their due recognition in a more constructive way than Augustine. Aquinas thought that we can have three kinds of virtues: perfect virtues, imperfect virtues, and false virtues. Naturally, perfect virtue is the goal that we have reason to strive for and, according to Aquinas, this is (in theory but not often in practice) possible only for Christians. Non-Christians can achieve imperfect virtues but, unlike Augustine, Aquinas does not think that these are in some way problematic. Although an imperfect virtue is incapable of putting God at the top of a hierarchy of value, this does not mean that a vice is in question. False virtues are possible for everyone: with these a person presents herself as virtuous but actually she carries out a vice. Here, unlike for imperfect virtues, it is a question of genuine vice. This distinction makes it possible for Aquinas also to commend non-Christians' virtues if they express genuine motivation, and he does not need, like Augustine, to relate sceptically to non-Christian good works.

Aquinas divides actual virtues into two classes: natural virtues and infused virtues. Natural virtues are justice (*iustitia*), courage (*fortitudo*), and temperance (*temperantia*).

12. On Aquinas' theory of virtues, see Stump, *Aquinas*, 307–89; McInerny, *Difficult Good*.

Practical wisdom or prudence (*prudentia*) is the controlling main virtue. Infused virtues are the theological virtues of faith (*fides*), hope (*spe*), and love (*caritas*). Natural virtues are natural because they increase (or weaken) as a consequence of a person's natural actions. Infused virtues do not depend on practice but are given to people as a divine gift, without practice.

When we discussed Aristotle, we noted that virtues correspond to a person's nature and essential being. Aquinas develops this thought in such a way that natural virtues correlate with a person's mental faculties, reason, will, and emotions. For Aquinas these mental faculties are all active when a person acts and makes choices. Wisdom guides people to evaluate their desires and to choose from them those that accord with reason. Justice guides a person toward the good of others, in accordance with reason. Patience and courage cause emotions to develop so that a person wants things that are reasonable.

Thomas recreates the classical thesis of the unity of virtues, but only in part. Whereas the classical thinkers were of the opinion that different virtues can be derived from other virtues, Aquinas' way of assigning the different virtues to different parts of the soul makes such a simplification impossible. Instead, Aquinas thinks that the different virtues are closely connected with each other. If a virtue is missing, the machine will work, but sputtering as it does.

When it comes to natural virtues, a person develops competence with repetition: here Aquinas follows Aristotle. The strength of a virtue is always in proportion to the amount of experience gained and they are by nature permanent character traits. You cannot suddenly lose them. In principle it is possible that a non-Christian would be able to excel in all the natural virtues. Aquinas has no reason to deny that a non-Christian can live an exemplary life that even Christians could imitate. Before Aquinas it was typical to call natural virtues political virtues, because they were considered to be signs of a good state. Aquinas dropped this term, however. Actually, only justice can be considered a virtue that relates to the state. Accordingly, all natural virtues are primarily good character traits of the individual.

In spite of all their virtues, a non-Christian is in a state of perdition without infused virtues: faith, hope, and love. A person receives these as a gift, by grace and without merit. The requirement for receiving the gift is not prowess in natural virtues. It is a case of a supernatural gift that partly corrects the consequences of sin and helps make right the perverted mental faculties of a person. A person now understands his correct relationship with God and starts to love him. Natural virtues also continue their growth, and as wisdom increases so does the ability to apply them.

Aquinas' categorization of virtues does not make possible a distinction in which natural virtues have to do only with the reality we know and theological virtues have to do only with spiritual life. Rather, Thomas sees human life as a whole. A person's interpersonal moral life cannot be separated from their relation with God, and the practice of theological virtues always has a public form.

Infused virtues can, however, bring about works that seem to be in contradiction with natural virtues. For example, if someone gives up their life for someone else, he could be considered foolhardy, but the infused virtue of love sometimes demands such a thing. In the same way, patience can have ascetic forms that are not meant for everyone. (Thomas thinks that practicing asceticism should not harm a person, however.)

After the Reformation, Protestants related reservedly toward the idea of infused virtues: what would they be needed for? The purpose of infused virtues is, however, to make sure that faith, by which a person believes, is really a person's own mental act. As an infused virtue, faith is a person's own faith. However, he would not have faith unless God granted it to him. Therefore virtue is an infused gift. Infused grace, however, makes it possible for a person's will to actively work in cooperation with the will of God. Human action and God's influence are not mutually exclusive.

Development and growth can and must take place with respect to infused virtues, as well. Unlike natural virtues, however, an infused virtue can be lost as a result of one wrong act; this requires a so-called deadly sin, in other words a conscious turning away from God. For example, falling into sin as a result of weakness of the will does not result in the loss of an infused virtue.

In addition to Aquinas wanting to give the virtues possessed by non-Christians the value they deserve, he embarks on reinstating Aristotle's concept of magnanimity in the wake of Augustine's critique. According to Aquinas, a magnanimous person tries to do great and good things, and thinks he is able to do these fine things, but not with the aim of gaining respect and not being self-sufficient. In Aquinas' view, what goes with magnanimity is the right kind of control of a person's sense of honor. It is actually a vice to underestimate oneself or not to recognise one's own gifts, abilities, and strengths. A magnanimous individual has a realistic self-image. He does great things, but for the benefit of others. The giving of gifts goes with Aristotle's magnanimity, such that the person becomes independent of others, which in turn leads to the opposite: others become dependent on him. For Aquinas, the giving of gifts does not result from applying economic principles but rather should be free and unsolicited. It also belongs within Christian magnanimity that a person not consider her gifts, abilities, and virtues something that they have earned themselves.

LATE SCHOLASTICISM AND HUMANISM

After Thomas, Duns Scotus and William of Ockham became the most influential thinkers. In their thinking the role of virtue is completely different. Thomas' model sounded too deterministic to their ears: against this they emphasized human freedom and moral responsibility. There is real freedom only when the will is *indifferent* or, in other words, when it could just as well choose any course of action. A habitual virtue steers a person toward particular choices, which a virtuous person does voluntarily and willingly. According to the so-called voluntaristic tradition, this removes, or at least significantly weakens, a person's moral responsibility for their actions.

In late-medieval moral theory, the viewpoint changes from the habituation of good character traits to internal reflection. Humility means the recognition of internal discord. The change of perspective is subtle but significant. Instead of an individual recognizing that his goodness is a gift and dependent on grace, he recognizes the difference between the reality and the ideal.

Whereas for Augustine and Thomas human action is founded on participation between a person and God, in voluntarism a person is a free agent with her own sphere of influence. An individual's salvation is on the basis of a particular covenant (*pactum*) between God and him. When a person does his own part, God grants grace as a response. Receiving grace does not, however, depend on any inherent value of the actions; rather, it is as if God considered the person's poor efforts to be better than they really are. In this connection the expression "To the one who does what lies within him, God does not deny his grace" was used, the original meaning of which was to emphasize a person's own responsibility for how he uses his will.

At the same time, however, human actions became separated from the habituation process and moral renewal. Eudaimonistic teleology no longer holds. Scotus notes how a Roman soldier gives his life for Rome without expecting a reward (or at least anything that would benefit him), just as in the same way a Christian's love for God should not involve the hope of a reward. Good works should be done because God so commands, not because we would benefit from them in any way. In the view of voluntarists, placing virtue within a habituation model takes away the unsolicited character of virtue.

Another current in the late-medieval period was humanism, and within it virtue is given yet another new role. Humanism is a very diverse movement but there are some commonalities among its different aspects. Erasmus of Rotterdam set about promoting a complete system of wise thought that brought together erudition and Christian spirituality. The real purpose of education is to change not only a person's thoughts but his whole personality. The key tool in this was rhetoric, which is for awakening a person's desire for imitation (*imitatio*): the desire to act in the same way as the greatest example of virtue, Christ.

Erasmus was horrified at the moral corruption in his own time, but his critique was not directed only at obvious and visible external crimes. Even worse than those were evil deeds that, from the outside, looked like virtues. The worst crime was pretended religious devotion that maintained external rituals but, inside, kept a distance. Although real virtue is always internal, Erasmus did not mean that it could not show on the outside or that the Church's rituals and participation in them were bad. Properly used, external matters enliven internal reality. Devotion to the saints should arouse in us a desire to imitate their acts. Without this internal impulse devotion would be useless and even harmful. In *In Praise of Folly* he writes, "for how many zealous votaries are there that pay so profound respect to the Virgin Mary, as to place lighted tapers even at noon day upon her altars? And yet how few of them copy after her untouched chastity, her modesty, and her other commendable virtues, in the imitation whereof consists the truest esteem of divine devotion?"[13]

All in all, Erasmus has quite a positive understanding of the human person. If only the right example is put in front of someone, he cannot help loving and imitating it. Virtue can be exercised. The possibility of hypocrisy does not bother Erasmus if the person's intention is good.

MARTIN LUTHER

The reformer Martin Luther's concept of virtues draws from late-medieval philosophy and theology, which he both criticizes and adopts. Luther's educational background was nominalist, so he came to adopt an at least partly critical approach to Aristotelian-Thomist habituation theory. In the same way as Erasmus he emphasized internal piety and criticized external rituals and inauthenticity.

For Luther, the fact that people are imperfect in many ways was not the worst thing, but rather that they do not recognize their true state. Hypocrisy was his main concern, and Luther saw dangerous ingredients of this in the Aristotelian-Thomist way of thinking. His main target of criticism is found in Aristotle's words: "a man becomes just by doing just actions and temperate by doing temperate actions; and no one can have the remotest chance of becoming good without doing them."[14] In Luther's opinion this kind of principle completely distorts the idea of righteous-

13. Erasmus, *In Praise of Folly*, 72.
14. NE 1105b.

ness by faith. For this reason he expresses grave judgement of Aristotle and Thomas. Regarding Aristotle, Luther does, however, admit that his philosophy is good philosophy and generally applicable to life, as long as it is not brought in as a part of theology and Christian soteriology. In Luther's opinion, Thomas is guilty of this error.

Luther relates negatively to the possibility of influencing a person by changing his external behavior. For him, various pious deeds start to look suspect because they can lead to a false religiosity. Luther brings back the force of Augustine's virtue critique. Human attempts to look good should be related to with great suspicion. In his lectures on the Letter to the Romans, he likened Israel's exodus to a journey from vices to virtues but notes how the Christian life is "an exodus from virtues to the grace of Christ."[15] With this, it would be natural to assume that he was unable to accord great value to good works done by non-Christians. However, he thinks that in a Christian culture it is natural for people to act according to the rules they have been taught and in this way to attain at least a certain level of righteousness. This does not have anything to do with a person's relationship with God, however.

Luther turned sharply against late-scholastic teaching that seemed to suggest that we earn our salvation and rejected the idea that a person can do anything to earn God's favor—even with God's help. In practice Luther therefore rejected both Scotus' and Ockham's covenant theology and the Aristotelian-Thomist compatibility model. Instead, Luther emphasizes complete human passivity. The Latin word *passio* means both suffering and being the object of action. Just as God rested on the seventh day, the Sabbath, so a person should rest: "that we not only cease from our labor and

15. WA 56:158; LW 25:136–37. Quoted in Herdt, *Putting on Virtue*, 176.

trade but much more—that we let God alone work in us and that in all our powers do we do nothing of our own."[16] God's work in developing people often happens through unpleasant events by which God makes a person humble and even humiliates him. Commenting on the Old Testament patriarchs' and prophets' foolish acts, Luther notes how God allows even his chosen ones to fall into sin so that they would not become proud.

Like Thomas, Luther emphasizes that God radically takes initiatives. A person cannot do anything to earn grace. However, this results in a problem that has traditionally been called the theologians' cross (*crux theologorum*), in other words a question that cannot be answered: why some people believe and others do not believe (*cur alii, alii non*).

There is some tension in Luther's teaching between a person's own activity and radical monergism, in other words God's omnipotence. Luther could not accept that a person might be passive in the sense that a log or a stone is. A person has a will, but he is able to use it only to resist. However, when someone has received grace, his will is corrected so that he is capable of cooperating with God.

> Why does God not do it all by himself, since he is able to help everyone and knows how to help everyone? Yes, he can do it; but he does not want to do it alone. He wants us to work with him. He does us the honor of wanting to effect his work with us and through us.[17]

In the end Luther comes very close to Aquinas. One difference, however, is the possibility of hypocrisy. Aquinas thinks that hypocrisy is not worth fearing too much, but for Luther this is one of the worst sins. Another difference

16. WA 6:244; LW 31:348. Herdt, *Putting on Virtue*, 176.
17. WA 6:52; LW 44:52. Herdt, *Putting on Virtue*, 186.

relates to the ontological status of infused virtue. According to Luther a person's genuine good works are done by Christ through him. In principle, Aquinas agrees but would emphasize the place of infused virtue, which guides a person's mental faculties in the right direction. As a nominalist, Luther sees no need for this, in his view, superfluous matter: if Christ can do this, for what would a person need any special infused virtue? In addition, not even a good work or virtue aided by infused virtue is necessarily sufficiently good for God, who demands perfection.

The problem in Luther's theology stems from an overemphasized demand for passivity together with an undeveloped theory of divine and human cooperation. He does not offer a rationally satisfying solution, but instead appeals to paradox and mystery. At the same time, nevertheless, Luther provides plenty of guidance for parents, spouses, children, teachers, pastors, and those in government. In this he sounds very Aristotelian. The teaching of a good life starts at home when children are small, and upbringing should take place in a loving environment. A child's best teacher is always her own parent. A child is bound to become like his company and environment, both in good and bad. Luther naturally teaches that it is better that an environment is virtuous. Despite this he has to give a warning of how this emphasis on outward virtue can lead people spiritually astray.

Luther tries to prevent a person from starting to take note of his own good works and virtues in the hope of winning favor with God and other people. His solution is, however, so extreme that the pendulum swings to the other side, and this can have just the same consequences as the hypocrisy that Luther feared. A person can start conforming to his own passivity, which prevents moral action. Why do good if it is really just a twisted attempt to look better than I really am?

JEAN-JACQUES ROUSSEAU

The Enlightenment and the streams of thought that followed it sent theorizing about virtue off in many different directions.[18] In the thought of Jean-Jacques Rousseau, a hyper-Augustinian view rose to new heights. Although Augustine's approach to human virtue was one of suspicion, according to him a person's good works are always by dint of God's grace and influence. Good works find their right place only if a person recognizes their dependence on others, especially on God. Luther, who follows Augustine in many aspects, emphasizes the Augustinian suspicion toward human motives. After the Enlightenment, confession of one's depravity takes the place of recognizing one's dependence on God. With Rousseau this step toward honesty turns everything upside down. He acknowledges a person's capability of being an agent, but the moral estimation of the nature of self changes dramatically. What for Luther was a source of shame (that which, deep down, I am) Rousseau puts forward as an example to follow.

Rousseau thought that in the history of humanity there had been a Fall from a natural state to a society. Originally, the human being was independent and free, a "noble savage", but he ends up mentally shackled when he lives and acts in a society. In Rousseau's view, the norms that society offers as virtues are actually vices and sources of false religion. He compares society to a theater in which people play different roles that do not represent what they really are. In Rousseau's thinking the essence of virtue is authenticity. A virtuous person is honestly what he really is.

18. Herdt, *Putting on Virtue*, 281–340.

Rousseau distinguishes between two different forms of self-love. The first is a good and natural desire to protect oneself (*l'amour de soi-même*). The other, corrupted form is loving oneself via the approval and opinion of others (*amour-propre*). Rousseau thinks that the Fall is precisely a move from natural self-love to corrupted self-love in which a person becomes bound to others in the wrong way. In his natural state a person did not compare himself to others or seek approval from them; in the natural state there was no theater, but existence was free of all pretense. According to Rousseau, all evil comes into the world as a result of the competition and comparison that accompanies wrong love. Rousseau also puts forward his very Lutheran-sounding critique of those who aim for ideals by claiming that, behind outwardly beautiful virtues, is often just corrupted *amour-propre*, which does good deeds to make the agent look good.

According to Rousseau, nobody is *virtuous* by nature, but a person is *good* by nature. Therefore a human does not need any special habituation in order to become good: she just needs to understand her own essential nature and expose it from under the dross society has piled on us. A person's natural virtue is crystalized in two virtues: the will to survive and pity. The will to survive is the right kind of self-love mentioned above, and pity is, according to Rousseau, an innate and automatic human reaction to suffering.

Rousseau's social criticism comes out clearly in the work *Emile*, in which he describes the education of a boy, Emile, completely outside the corrupt influence of society. A central pedagogical principle is to avoid having anything to do with other people. The ideal state for Rousseau is to be alone and independent. In *Emile*, Rousseau gives a harsh judgement of Aristotelian habituation thought: "The only habit the child should be allowed to acquire is to contract none."[19] In Rousseau's thought, habituation is connected with the loss of freedom, the external observance of rules and subservience to someone else's power. Paradoxically Emile ends up submitting to his teacher's (that is, Rousseau's) authority in order to learn independence. Similarly, this state of isolation is hardly one that could be called natural in any way.

Rousseau is, however, unsure about how Emile will turn out. When he eventually comes to have contact with other people, will he also be corrupted? One way of resolving this that Rousseau suggests is that Emile should be made to encounter suffering first, which will bring out his natural virtue of pity. In this way pity can be put before envy, which Emile would eventually come across when he meets people who have grown up in society.

Rousseau nevertheless has another route to independence and it is the central theme of his *Confessions*. Rousseau attempts to offer a path to authenticity to those to whom the kind of upbringing that Emile got is no longer possible. If honesty and encountering one's real self was something painful and eventually shameful to Luther, Rousseau recognizes the difficulty of this process but considers the end result to be more a victory for defiance and pride than an indication of regret. In *Confessions* Rousseau sets about opening up his own life as fully as possible. There are two purposes to this act of honesty. On the one hand, its purpose is to put Rousseau in a position in which he exists as an individual unlike others and is therefore of value. On the other hand, he tries to awaken the same kind of honesty in others, too.

It is clear, however, that, his autobiographical style is also a way of seeking justification. The consequence is a paradoxical situation: Rousseau strives for independence

19. Rousseau, *Emilé, or on Education*, 63.

and freedom from other's approval but he nevertheless seeks approval (for example by offering reasons why he gave up his own child to an orphanage). Aiming to be an independent subject, Rousseau is perhaps a bit too interested in what others think of him.

DAVID HUME

In David Hume's thinking a certain version of Aristotelian virtue theory makes a return. In Aristotle's thought, a teleology is central, in which the goal of a person's deeds serves as the starting point for assessing the virtuousness of those deeds. Hume gives up teleology and in this way the definition of good becomes an increase in self-knowledge and reflection on one's own actions, instead of a growth process and habituation. Virtue is faithfulness to what a human is, in a slightly similar way to how Rousseau thought.

Hume's virtue ethics is, however, openly hostile to Christian virtue ethics. Whereas Christians typically thought that particular desires, and virtues, are forces that have to be bridled, cultivated, and constantly related to each other so that they do not become vices, Hume approaches the matter out of a positive anthropology: virtues are, in fact, natural desires and for this reason good in themselves. Pride is the central virtue and humility is listed amongst vices. By pride, Hume means the satisfaction that comes about when an individual sees in himself something that he feels is of value. The purpose of pride is to reinforce the sense of oneself and strengthen an individual's identity. Pride should be expressed to the right degree, however. Both excessive and too little pride lead to self-deceit. Moreover, pride should be concealed from other people, otherwise it will work against the individual.

Pride also functions as a motivator for doing good. Hume recognizes how objects of pity and sympathy are found more easily from nearby than from afar; we protect our own more than those far away. Nevertheless, it is pride that can make us do good to those outside our own circle. Honor and magnanimity motivate people to do good even to those who do not belong to the same family.

Like Rousseau, Hume thinks that goodness is inherent in people. Although people often have selfish motives, in the end they are more good than bad. In their natural state, humans are able to be virtuous only toward their own family and circle. People do not have innate passion, morally motivating emotion, toward such an abstract target as "human race." A moral upbringing and guidance are needed in order for a person to love a society or community larger than his family.

Why should I love a larger community anyway? Hume says that a virtuous life generates more satisfaction than one of vice. In this way he belongs partly in the eudaimonistic tradition. The great problem in discussion of Hume, however, has been whether to see Hume's position as one of loving virtue as an end in itself or only as a means to happiness.

Unlike Christian philosophers, Hume does not think that we should be particularly concerned about the motivation behind virtues. This is relatively self-evident since, for Hume, seeking honor is basically a good thing. Thinking like this, it is difficult to come up with a way in which the motivation could be especially bad. In Hume's view, it is Christian virtue that is problematic. The reason is the inauthenticity of Christianity, because it forces upon people a model that does not naturally suit them. Christian humility is, in Hume's opinion, against human nature. Furthermore, it leads to problematic end results, such as an inability to value virtue that is expressed separately from Christian faith and general denial of life.

With regard to Hume (and also Rousseau), we see how different thinkers use virtues in very different ways. When attempts have been made to create new ways of working with the help of virtues, critics have noted how one person's virtue is another's vice. Is Hume's interpretation of pride therefore completely different from, for instance, Aquinas, who integrated magnanimity with humility? Although Hume intends to create a consciously non-Christian moral theory, even he is unable, in reality, to move far away from Aquinas. Aquinas too recognizes false humility and the lack of a sense of self-worth, which Hume mistakenly takes to be the Christian ideal. Also, Aquinas' definition of magnanimity is not very different from Hume's. The largest difference between Hume and Christian virtue ethics concerns the unity of virtues. Hume settles for less, when Christians think that virtues should make up a larger whole.

IMMANUEL KANT

In the history of recent philosophy, Immanuel Kant has had the role of being a strong defender of deontological ethics, and he is not generally considered to be especially interested in virtues: what is essential is that a deed is done on the basis of general moral law, not on the basis of the characteristics of the agent. Although Kant distances himself from the Aristotelian tradition, he nevertheless retains quite a lot of it.

Kant defines a virtue as the ability by which the will fulfils the responsibility given to it. Kant thinks that prior to a virtue there is a moral rule and responsibility. Good is therefore not derived from what a virtuous, practically wise person would do, but from what is reasonable. Neither does Kant treat virtue as a second nature but rather more as a particular ability, willpower, which helps a person to do what his reason recommends.

Kant does not leave the character completely out of it, though. In *Groundwork of the Metaphysics of Morals* (393/7) he states, "Nothing in the world—or out of it!—can possibly be conceived that could be called 'good' without qualification except a GOOD WILL. Mental talents such as intelligence, wit, and judgment, and temperaments such as courage, resoluteness, and perseverance are doubtless in many ways good and desirable; but they can become extremely bad and harmful if the person's character isn't good—i.e. if the will that is to make use of these gifts of nature isn't good."

In this way he acknowledges the characteristics of the moral agent. If we ask what "good will" means, though, we get the answer: a good will is in line with moral law. Thus moral law is always more fundamental than the will that observes it. Kant is especially interested in the ability of our reason to recognise moral law—and the reasonableness of this law is the real reason for acting according to it. Here he is quite close to Aristotle's emphasis, according to which virtue should always be chosen as an end in itself, not because there is an even greater good behind it.

According to Kant, something that is right should be done only because it is right, and because it is therefore a person's duty. If other motives are at play, there is cause to doubt the purity of the deed. In this respect, Kant's thinking is reminiscent of Augustinian-Lutheran anxiety and late scholastic theology. This is also the source of Kant's criticism of eudaimonism. By his interpretation, eudaimonism means that good and right are not chosen for their own sakes but for the sake of the happiness they produce. However, this is a mistaken interpretation of classical eudaimonism, in which virtue and happiness are ends in themselves. His interpretation being what it is, though, Kant criticizes Hume's position, in which good is seen expressly as an instrument for achieving happiness.

Although Kant follows Augustine in his demand for purity, he does not accept Augustine's definition of God as the goal of good deeds. According to Kant, beyond moral law there is nothing. Augustine thinks that God, one whose characteristics make him perfect, is the sum of moral law: law in itself is not fully good, only God is. Even though superficially the difference is quite small, Kant's criticism of traditional metaphysics makes him draw limits that put him in opposition to Christian thinkers and lead him to use definitions that are not easily compatible with each other. This becomes especially evident in his attempts to define a person as a subject of virtue. Kant's anthropology determines, on the one hand, his concept of radical evil (people are more evil than good) and, on the other hand, his idea of radical autonomy (a person and only a person is the subject of her actions). A person's evil becomes apparent especially in his inability to produce pure deeds, which, in effect, means that all his acts are bad in some way. This can be for three different reasons. First, a person can be weak and suffer from a weak will (*akrasia*): he would like to act rightly but is unable. Second, although a person might act rightly, his motive is not necessarily pure but influenced by factors other than a plain desire to obey law. Third, a person can suffer from a distortion such that he does good openly from bad motives, such as for the sake of honor or thanks.

From this starting point, how do we get to the situation in which a person, by their own strength, aims toward the good? Kant suggests that Christ offers an example to be followed. However, to retain human autonomy, he cannot accept (unlike, Augustine and Aquinas, for example) that

God aids the human will. Kant's anti-metaphysical theology does admit some supernatural assistance, but only to a very minor degree. He does, in an Augustinian style, speak of the need for a change of mind and conversion, but in the end the status of this conversion remains unclear. According to Jennifer Herdt, in Kant's thought a Pelagian concept of the will is joined with an Augustinian concept of sin, and the result is aporia, perplexity.[20]

FRIEDRICH NIETZSCHE

Nietzsche's name does not first spring to mind when talking about virtues. What we have already said about Rousseau and Hume helps us to understand, however, how broadly virtue can be understood. Among modern thinkers, whereas Kant wants to move to the left and retain key elements of the medieval virtue tradition, Nietzsche veers to the right and declares that medieval Christian moral theorizing is degenerate. As if this was not enough, Plato and Aristotle have in his opinion turned away from the genuine Hellenistic way of thinking. Therefore Nietzsche suggests a return to heroic virtues: "My distrust of Plato is fundamental. I find him so very much astray from all the deeper instincts of the Hellenes, so steeped in moral prejudices, so pre-existently Christian—the concept 'good' is already the highest value with him."[21] In this way we have come full circle and, in a way, returned to our starting point.

Nietzsche's works are aphoristic and do not follow a systematic style of presentation, so his theory of virtue is undeniably difficult to get a hold of. On the other hand, one can find critical comments on various individual virtues in his works. In *Gay Science* he states, "Virtues (such

20. Herdt, *Putting on Virtue*, 322–40.
21. Nietzsche, *Twilight of the Idols and the Anti-Christ*, 117.

as diligence, obedience, chastity, piety, justice) are mostly harmful to their possessors. . . . When you have a virtue . . . you are its *victim*." At the same time, he picks a variety of virtues and gives them new definitions. In *The Antichrist* (2) he proclaims,

> What is good?—All that heightens the feeling of power, the will to power, power itself in man. What is bad?—All that proceeds from weakness. What is happiness?—The feeling that power increases—that a resistance is overcome. Not contentment, but more power, not peace at all, but war; not virtue, but proficiency (virtue in the Renaissance style, *virtu*, virtue free of moralic acid.

For Nietzsche, virtue has a certain relationship with desire. As is well-known, desire is for Nietzsche a will to power (*Wille zur Macht*), which is the force that drives human action. Virtue is the ideal epitome of this will and desire.

What virtues are in question in Nietzsche's case? In Nietzsche's thought the ideal moral example and the epitome of virtue is naturally "the superhuman" who partly displays features of Aristotle's magnanimity. The superhuman's main virtue is solitude and independence. He gets opposition for his actions everywhere and constantly clashes with the large masses. The superhuman has no wish for reconciliation nor does he seek peace, and his relationship to other individuals is solely instrumental; he only has to do with others when they can in some way be of benefit to him and his own purposes.

The superhuman does not withdraw but takes ambitious initiatives: he wants to leave a mark. However, in this way the superhuman, as already stated, gets enemies and opposition. In these situations, and whenever he suffers failure, he displays fortitude, by which he rises up straight away. Nietzsche calls this "health," which does not refer to physical health but rather to the attitude that the superhuman has toward sickness and weakness: he is indomitable. The superhuman is not furtive and does not underrate or doubt himself, his achievements or abilities. The "Dionysian attitude to life" is connected with being steadfast. The superhuman accepts his life as it is, and he is ready to live it again in the same way, without regret (this is what Nietzsche means with the thought of "eternal return").

What has just been described does not, however, mean closed-mindedness or an uncritical stance. Nietzsche emphasizes how a virtuous life is extremely harsh and demanding. Nietzsche's philosophy is often called agonistic, painful. The pain results from a certain epistemic, or intellectual, attitude, which drives the superhuman toward the truth. A fundamental intellectual virtue for Nietzsche is curiosity, which notably the Christian virtue tradition has considered a vice. For example, Aquinas thinks that curiosity is a vice if someone tries to deal with something that is beyond his intellect or if he consciously serves an evil goal.[22] For Nietzsche, however, the desire for knowledge is a virtue, and he wants to underline this with his interpretation of curiosity. Nietzschean curiosity is an unquenchable thirst for knowledge that does not shun difficult questions nor is satisfied with easy answers.

Curiosity also requires courage. Asking the wrong questions can result in anger in those who do not like established ideas to be questioned. Another virtue that aims at the same end is honesty. Only a courageous and honest person is able to look at himself directly in the mirror. Courage is also required because, according to Nietzsche, knowledge about our own selves is often not very pleasant.

22. ST II-II, 167

QUESTIONS FOR CONSIDERATION

1. How did Augustine change ancient virtue theorization?

2. How did Aquinas challenge Augustine's thinking on the virtues?

3. What are typical features of Enlightenment-era reflection on the virtues?

4. How can Nietzsche be considered a virtue theorist?

3

VIRTUES AND VICES

THE LIST OF BOTH virtues and vices is very long. It would be quite easy to list several dozen of them. It is not necessary for us to go through all virtues and vices, or even the most important, here. In this chapter we will look at the four traditional cardinal virtues (temperance, courage, justice, wisdom) and the three theological virtues (faith, hope, love). Study of these virtues and their corresponding vices shows how they are dependent on each other, how the different virtues support one another, and how lack of one virtue prevents realization of another. In this overview I will make use of Thomas Aquinas' definitions in particular, because in his *Summa Theologica* he offers a broad view of the various virtues that have long been influential in the history of Western thought.[1]

---

1. In addition I have found especially useful the relevant chapters from Peterson and Seligman, *Character Strengths*, and Timpe and Boyd, *Virtues and Their Vices*. The empirical studies I refer to, and many others, can be found in the first of these books.

CARDINAL VIRTUES

Temperance

As a virtue, temperance can mean many different things. A temperate person is long-suffering and relates to others' faults with gentleness; she is patient and forgiving. She is satisfied with her own part and what she has; she is humble and modest. A temperate person is able, nevertheless, to enjoy her life and actively seek enjoyment, but in moderation. She does not drink or party too much and she does not let the happiness of the moment prevent happiness in the future. A temperate person is also a realist, neither a pessimist nor an optimist.

In visual art, temperance is often depicted as a woman who has a jar of wine in her hand. This portrays the ability to apportion things in just the right amount. Temperance often refers to self-control, and this has been the basic interpretation of classical and Christian thinkers in particular. For example, according to Aquinas, temperance refers to how someone's passions should not come to determine his actions beyond what reason permits.

Psychologists have observed how an ability to display temperance and other virtues linked with it correlates positively with various good life experiences. Accordingly, excessive rigorousness or an inability to restrain oneself leads to negative outcomes regarding wellbeing. For example, people who have good self-control succeed better in demanding working conditions, for example in the academic world. Those who can keep themselves in check suffer less from depression, anxiety, and many other mental disturbances. Also, thinking intuitively, temperance makes everyday situations easier.

Imagine a situation in which a father is trying to teach his child to eat with a spoon. In the early stages of practicing, the mashed potato flies around the room, but soon the spoon starts to find its way into the child's mouth and there is a decrease in the amount of cleaning needed. If the father sets out on this project with an attitude of temperance (he has a realistic idea of what the child is capable of, and he does not try to feed a child who is already full or tired, and so on), he will have more success and everyone will feel better. If, instead, he is impatient and his expectations are unrealistic, everybody suffers in the end.

How can temperance be learned? It is clear that cultural factors have some influence. For example, in some cultures people may drink large quantities of alcohol but alcoholism is nevertheless a rather rare phenomenon. This combination is possible if the culture includes the idea that getting drunk is a bad and embarrassing thing, and the idea that an individual is always morally responsible for his actions, whether he drinks or not. Certain studies have also observed that the number of teenage pregnancies in a society correlates with its distance from the equator: in warm countries sexual restraint is more difficult. Therefore, context does have an influence on our actions even if it does not rule out our own decisions.

The mystical concept called willpower is often associated with temperance. Contrary to what is often thought, willpower does not seem to be like a muscle, which can be strengthened through training. Willpower is more or less constant, like a you-are-freed-from-prison playing card that you can use only once during the game. For this reason, someone wanting to develop temperance in relation to eating or drinking, for example, has to plan their actions in advance. If I want to lose weight, I should choose to have lunch at a salad bar, not a cake shop where I will be vulnerable to temptation. Someone struggling with alcoholism should not go into a bar even to meet friends. Someone who is short-tempered does well to go through in his mind beforehand how he will act when he exceeds his annoyance threshold ("if the child throws a spoonful of mash at the wall, I will walk into another room for a moment and ask my spouse to continue feeding the child"). Temperance comes about through routines by which we avoid getting into difficult situations in which we know we will choose wrongly. The choice should be made much earlier than when the situation is upon us.

A lack of temperance leads to an inability to enjoy life. A lifestyle that is too puritanical deprives oneself and others of joy. Similarly, intemperance leads to joylessness. It is not a constant increase in stimuli that makes one happy, but the right kind of variation. For example, after a few months of fasting from chocolate, a small piece of chocolate tastes wonderful.

How should we think about addiction from the standpoint of the virtue of temperance? Is an alcoholic or drug addict intemperate? In my opinion, no, although the line can often be thin. An alcoholic suffers from weakness of the will, not intemperance. An alcoholic wants to stop drinking but an intemperate person does not; an intemperate person enjoys (at least to start with) exaggerated enjoyment. Intemperance is not about the amount, either, but about one's intentions. For example, Uncle Scrooge may in his own opinion be temperate in his stinginess, but he is motivated by greed for money, not wisdom or a desire to find a balance between different virtues. In the same way an extreme exercise junkie may in his own opinion be very virtuous and capable of keeping himself in check, but if exercising is motivated by, for example, a twisted body image, it is a vice.

Courage

The virtue of courage is easily associated with war and other extreme situations. Historically this is the background out of which this virtue arises. In Plato's *Republic*, courage was expressly the virtue of soldiers. In *Beowulf*, heroes are described in a way that underlines the unity of virtues: a real soldier is not just brave but also honest and just.[2]

> Thus Beowulf bore himself with valor;
> he was formidable in battle yet behaved with honor
> and took no advantage; never cut down
> a comrade who was drunk, kept his temper
> and, warrior that he was, watched and controlled
> his God-sent strength and his outstanding
> natural powers.
>
> (lines 2177–83; tr. Heaney)

Awareness of inevitable death is a key element in heroic bravery. The last words of Beowulf, fatally wounded by a dragon, are:

> "You are the last of us, the only one left
> of the Waegmundings. Fate swept us away,
> sent my whole brave high-born clan
> to their final doom. Now I must follow them."
> That was the warrior's last word.
> He had no more to confide. The furious heat
> of the pyre would assail him. His soul fled from his breast
> to its destined place among the steadfast ones.
>
> (lines 2814–20; tr. Heaney)

Absolute and active engagement in a situation in which there is no hope and in which death is the only

---

2. McInerny, "Fortitude and the Conflict of Frameworks."

expected result is typical of the courage of a classical hero. Complete lack of hope is what makes a heroic act perfect.

Courage is also needed, though, in other places than on the battlefield. In the Middle Ages, courage was treated as a part of theory of action: what kind of act displays genuine courage? By definition there is always a risk associated with courage. A deed is courageous if doing it endangers something that the agent values. In this connection a deed can mean a concrete act, or something that is said, that changes something in the world, or a decision to remain in the situation in which the person already is.

Aquinas' definition of courage contains two pairs of concepts. First, magnanimity (*magnanimitas*) means trusting that an individual is able to achieve something significant by her action, and magnificence (*magnificentia*) refers to the quality of the act. Second, patience (*patientia*) means ability to be hopeful in a situation in which there is no sign of hope. Perseverance (*perseverantia*) ensures that a person does not give up his hopes even under heavy pressure. According to Aquinas, what distinguishes courage is also that the courageous act is directed against something evil. The dangerous and foolish acts of a gullible person, for example, or acts involving great risk that are done in the hope of external benefit, cannot actually be considered courageous.

Courage is also a key intellectual virtue in that courage is manifested in the desire to know the truth and it is a fight against ignorance. Expressing opinions often requires courage and many scientific breakthroughs have required the character traits listed by Aquinas.

But when should one be courageous? It is clear that there are situations when we can act foolhardily or without consideration. For example, a person who denies the Holocaust could, in a way, be considered courageous. Courage in itself does not, however, say anything about the value of the act or whether the opinion that has courageously been brought forth is true. Therefore an individual needs to carefully consider where and when to display courage. The case of the Holocaust denier is an example of epistemic vice. He is driven by another value or goal (in this case, often antisemitism), which influences his assessment of evidence that supports the historicity of the Holocaust. This does not, however, mean that he does not have fortitude, something that is a good thing in itself. Nevertheless, in this case, where unity of the virtues is lacking, his fortitude is serving the wrong purpose.

According to a general definition, it is worth being courageous when the benefit of what is achieved though the courageous act will outweigh the associated risk. Furthermore, courage requires unity of the virtues: a courageous person must not be guilty of neglecting another virtue. If a person has not been sufficiently virtuous intellectually, he can courageously support completely crazy ideas, and the outcome will be one best described as a vice. In this way a person falls into a vice that could be called fanaticism or foolhardiness. A person suffering from lack of courage is timid or a coward. Genuine courage is therefore found in the region between, on the one hand, excessive self-criticism and timidity and, on the other hand, unthinking fanaticism. These extremes underline the reflective character of courage and the unity of virtues. Someone who is courageous in the right way is inevitably also wise.

Courage often leads people into problematic situations in which they come under many pressures. They can experience loneliness, discrimination, anxiety, and economic hardship. Generally, people who are exceptionally courageous are quite resilient regarding these. For example, in research on soldiers decorated for their bravery, it has been observed how they are typically hardened in character in many ways. They are psychologically mature and they have good self-confidence and balanced emotional lives. The courageous are often very intelligent and they are able to evaluate risks correctly. The role of the community in developing the virtue of courage also appears to be very significant. A courageous person greatly values the people around her and the community that she serves, and for this reason is ready to make big personal sacrifices.

Justice

"To everyone what he deserves," goes an old definition of justice. But what does it mean in practice? The difficulty of defining justice is emphasized by the macabre fact that the definition just given (Ger. *Jedem das Seine*) was written in iron letters above the gate of Buchenwald concentration camp. What is in question is: who is deserving and by whose criteria are we to judge?

It is natural to approach justice from the point of view of the dialectic between an individual and a community. Justice is a kind of harmony. I am in harmony with myself when my mental faculties, reason, and emotions are in balance. A harmonious community is composed of harmonious individuals. We think it is unjust if someone dictates to us how we should live. Therefore autonomy belongs to the idea of justice. However, if we live in a community, we cannot be completely autonomous but have to bargain for what, in our opinion, belongs to us.

Justice is in that sense a negative and passive virtue, in that we can be just without doing anything: we let others do whatever they want in peace. However, if we see injustice in the world, virtue demands action. In this connection we can talk of righteous anger that both motivates an individual to act and challenges others to change their way of acting. When does justice manifest itself in anger? Many skilled orators and human rights activists have skillfully used strong language to express the ideal of justice. A well-known example is Martin Luther King's famous "I Have a Dream" speech, in which he points his finger directly at the Governor of Alabama while talking about the State's "vicious racists" and how the Governor's lips are "dripping with the words of interposition and nullification." Why does this angry part not define King's speech? Because it is just one sentence in the middle of a long speech, the aim of which lies elsewhere. The negative and critical point is overshadowed by the otherwise positive message. The same sentence continues and ends with the hope that "one day right there in Alabama little black boys and black girls will be able to join hands with little white boys and white girls as sisters and brothers."

In one of his other speeches ("Showdown for Nonviolence") King instructs his listeners to choose between constructive nonviolence and rioting. According to King, anger smouldering under the surface can be defused in a way that can be for everyone's best, but it has to be channelled correctly. Zag Cogley suggests that there are two ways one can fail in expressing just anger.[3] First, injustices should evoke feelings of anger in us. If we do not feel anger in the right situations, we suffer from the vice of indifference. Second, if we are unable to communicate our anger rightly, we are guilty of wrath. A person who is under the control of wrath may suffer from moral superiority or pride. It is certainly quite possible that the wrath is a response to a real wrong. The problem is, however, that approaching the issue in this way, an enraged person just propagates and increases violence. The feeling may in itself be justified but the method

3. Cogley, "A Study of Virtuous and Vicious Anger."

for expressing it is wrong and prevents the enraged person from achieving his own goals.

Cogley presents three ways to recognize wrath, that is, anger that is a vice. First, wrath is expressed in situations in which it is inappropriate. Cultures differ from each other in their rules regarding this, so it is worth being sensitive. Second, wrath is by nature impulsive and uncontrolled. It is not an expression of the consideration and clear thinking that would enable the person listening to clearly recognize the reason for the anger. Third, wrath breaks relationships between members of the community. The speaker can, with his actions, create various cliques, demonize others, and encourage others to do dirty work on their behalf. Thus angry speech in reality aims to deepen the conflict, not to resolve it.

Virtuous anger displays an understanding of how communities work. To put it another way, a person does not just react with her own emotions to an unjust situation, but she responds to the situation holistically and, even when speaking angrily, aims at reconciliation, as King's example shows.

Wisdom

At the beginning of this book, we started out with Aristotle's definition of wisdom, according to which a young person may be talented in many ways, but not practically wise, because wisdom requires experience, and experience requires time. Wisdom is therefore different from intelligence. An extremely intelligent person can simultaneously be extremely stupid and morally corrupt. A wise person does not need to be highly intelligent. For example, German doctors at the beginning of last century were certainly very smart, but the way they related uncritically to eugenics and the use of prisoners in concentration camps as test subjects does not present a flattering picture of their character. At the same time, it is possible that a farmer with little schooling but a lot of life experience would have been able to see the problems involved in such scientific work.

In literature and film, wisdom is usually represented by elderly people, whose advice is typically a little enigmatic (J. R. R. Tolkien's fantasy characters Gandalf and Galadriel are examples of this). The purpose of this is to emphasise the difficulty that is connected with wisdom. Even if we were told what wisdom is in each situation, we would not recognize it as wisdom if we were not in some way receptive to it and able to understand what is in question. This difficulty is depicted via the character of Professor Dumbledore in the Harry Potter books. Harry does not understand Dumbledore's thoughts before he becomes part of them, sees things through his eyes, and *experiences* what Dumbledore is talking about.

Wisdom is typically something that results in others' benefit. A wise person is able to advise and guide others to live better. Also, by her own actions she shows consideration and all other virtues. In the Aristotelian tradition, wisdom is the highest virtue, which regulates the other virtues. Wisdom connects right thinking to right action. According to Aquinas, practical wisdom "is of good counsel about matters regarding [a person's] entire life, and the end of human life."[4] What is in question is the ability to find the golden mean between the vice of two extremes. Unlike for all the other virtues, the vice of immoderation does not apply to wisdom. Nobody can be too wise, in other words too good at finding the middle way between vices. A person can therefore grow in wisdom without limit. Wisdom applies to particular and contingent moments that never repeat

4. ST I-II, q. 57, a. 4, o.3

themselves in the same way. Therefore wisdom cannot only be knowledge of various rules and principles, but the ability to adapt them in just the right way. It is, for example, possible for a person to know and accept a recommendation "we must be just" but be unable to recognise what action really is just and what is not.

Lack of wisdom is, of course, called stupidity. A stupid person is unable to relate what he knows to larger wholes, nor to correctly evaluate the consequences of his actions. He lacks the necessary intellectual and moral virtues that would make right thinking and action possible. Stupidity is generally considered to be a self-imposed quality, when a person deliberately directs his action toward secondary goods and lets irrational desires control him.

According to Aquinas, wisdom is made up of three parts: deliberation (*eubulia*), decision (*synesis*), and action (*gnome*). Communality, in other words asking others for advice, belongs necessarily within wise deliberation. In order for a person to ask someone for advice, humility and the ability to learn are required. Aquinas states how someone hungry for wisdom "must carefully, frequently and reverently apply his mind to the teachings of the learned, neither neglecting them through laziness, nor despising them through pride."[5]

Wisdom also includes the ability to make a decision at the right time. This decision should display the understanding that comes with deliberation. Decision-making requires courage and the ability to fight against the vices of timidity or perfectionism. (A perfectionist is not able to make choices because in his opinion he has never prepared things well enough.) In the end, the action in itself must be realized in a way that broadly displays other virtues. A decision is stuck to, its basis is made transparent to others, and

5. ST II-II.49.3. a 2.

those to whom the matter is relevant are helped to move toward a good goal.

Of all virtues, wisdom is the most difficult to learn because it requires time and experience. Wisdom is learned by growing in all other virtues and making choices, including bad ones. Therefore you cannot just start to be wise; it is a goal that is unavoidably quite distant. So far, wisdom has not been studied much in psychological research, and it is obviously extremely difficult to measure the amount of wisdom. However, it is possible to estimate, for example, a person's ability to take different perspectives and viewpoints into account, and the ability to put oneself in someone else's position. These are abilities that can be influenced by training, for instance, but that is quite hard work and requires long periods of time. Among other research, it has been observed in studies carried out in the United States that teaching history from the viewpoint of the indigenous peoples has increased the ability of the test group to put things into perspective. In the same way, reading novels that describe complex and unpredictable human relationships has, at least momentarily, increased test subjects' ability to recognise various emotional states. However, the weight of the evidence from these kinds of tests based on conditioning is quite low. Although it could be proven that conditioning does work in certain contexts, we have no information about how long-lasting or permanent these influences are.

THEOLOGICAL VIRTUES

Faith

In ordinary speech, faith is often contrasted with knowledge in such a way as to imply that faith is in some way inferior to knowledge: if you do not have knowledge, you only have faith. In this usage, faith is mainly associated with an assumption, a guess, or even self-deception. The theological way of talking about faith, however, differs fundamentally from this ordinary use. Faith cannot be limited to the epistemic meaning described above. Instead, it typically means a whole attitude toward something that someone already considers true (in other words, that he *knows*).

Aquinas sees the relationship between faith, hope, and love as a kind of process in which one gives rise to the next: faith makes hope possible, and hope, love. He divides faith into three parts: *credere deo, credere Deum, credere in Deum.* The first part of faith means belief that God exists; God is the formal object of faith. The second part means the material contents of faith: those things that are believed about God. The third part means trust that all this is true, which makes the individual direct his life toward the highest good. The first two parts belong to the intellect and the third to the will. Therefore the first two parts are linked with the evaluation of whether something can justifiably be considered credible. In this way, faith and knowledge are not opposites:

> For since to believe is an act of the intellect assenting to the truth at the command of the will, two things are required that this act may be perfect: one of which is that the intellect should infallibly tend to its object, which is the true; while the other is that the will should be infallibly directed to the last end, on account of which it assents to the true: and both of these are to be found in the act of living faith. For it belongs to the very essence of faith that the intellect should ever tend to the true, since nothing false can be the object of faith.[6]

6. ST II-II 4. 5. Resp.

Without this kind of knowledge of the goodness and truthfulness of its object, faith would, in Aquinas' opinion, be a vice. In this way, faith is, or contains, intellectual virtue.

The third part of faith means, in practice, love, which gives faith its proper form. In this connection, Aquinas talks of faith formed by love (*fides charitate formata*). This love is needed in order for faith to be perfect. Without love, faith would be like an empty shell or an intention that never becomes concrete in actions. The central characteristic of love is its ability to connect two people together. Thus love means (among other things) the deep attitude that at best exists between lovers. Therefore, faith in its proper form can be considered a moral virtue.

In theological virtue theory, faith is usually described as an infused virtue. In other words, a person cannot obtain faith by trying or by exercising belief, but it is given as a gift. However, infused faith can and should deepen and strengthen, and how faith manifests itself in each individual is naturally reflected in that person's typical characteristics and existing natural virtues. Thus one person may have more knowledge than another person, and yet another person may express her faith through gentleness better than someone else.

Faith formed by love can lose its status as a virtue if a person commits a deadly sin, in other words a deliberately evil act that he does not regret. Unlike for natural virtues, even one of these kinds of acts can cause the loss of an infused virtue. Thus a person may still have an external habit of believing, but it has lost its inner power. The person can fall even deeper into sin than this if he develops inclinations that express hostility toward faith. In that case, the habitus of faith is replaced with disbelief. In the intellect, distrust, and in the will, malevolence, can take the place of faith. In this way, faith includes faithfulness toward the object of faith. Faith does not remain if its object is doubted or not respected.

Hope

As we noted in our discussion of courage, lack of hope was a fundamental part of the ideal of heroic courage. Ultimately, only the kind of sacrifice that is without hope is virtuous. Aristotle considered hope a typical passion of young people and did not see anything particularly virtuous about it. It was not until the influence of Christianity that hope joined the list of virtues.

Hope is fundamentally linked with action. According to Aquinas, even an animal understands hope. For example, if a dog sees a rabbit very far away it does not try to chase it, but if the rabbit is near, it attacks it, because it understands that then there is hope of catching it. In the same way, people's actions are directed toward purposes that are achievable. The object of hope is the forthcoming good. Hope always aims at some forthcoming state of affairs that is considered possible in some way. So a cognitive element always belongs to hope in the same way as it does to faith. I have to have some degree of assurance that what I am aiming for is good and true.

The vice that corresponds to hope is, of course, hopelessness (*desperatio*). Aquinas holds hopelessness to be an especially dangerous vice because it blocks human action and eventually removes the desire to exist at all. On the other hand, fanaticism, or excessive hope that does not correspond to reality, in the end leads to cynicism, which itself is one form of hopelessness. A person can also end up becoming entangled in sensory reality to the extent that higher goods do not interest him any longer and he does not strive toward anything that he does not yet have, but becomes satisfied with what he currently has. This is a consequence of listlessness (*acedia*), which also leads to hopelessness. Thus a person loses hope because he no longer holds that the object of hope is possible.

According to Aquinas, fear is connected with hope, just as it is with faith: someone who hopes for something good also fears the kind of bad in the future that could make realization of the hope impossible. For Aquinas, fear is something positive, promoting the person's best, because it guides the person's action in the right direction and requires thought.

Love

Love as a virtue is fundamentally connected with the concept of *eudaimonia*. By nature we want happiness; nobody needs to teach or command us to aim for it. Where we think happiness can be found varies, of course, and the object of our desire makes our life unique to us. This highest goal is something that we aim at for its own sake (not because, by it, we could achieve some other good). The goal is something that we think will make maximum satisfaction possible. Aquinas lists the typical highest goods we love as, among others, wealth, honor, power, physical wellbeing, and sensual pleasures. According to him, all of these things are good in themselves and, rightly managed, an essential part of human life. However, none of them can, in the end, be the highest good, because each of them is in itself deficient in some way.

From this starting point, Aquinas begins to construct his theory about the virtue of love. In everyday language, love is synonymous with the emotion, but the theological use again differs significantly from everyday usage. Love as a virtue is not an emotion but a willingness to act for the best of the other. Many kinds of emotions can certainly be associated with love (of which only some are pleasant) but no particular emotion is necessary for love to actually exist. I can say I love someone only if I want their best. If I do not have this attitude, I can, at most, want or desire someone. There is not inevitably anything bad in this desire. A person by nature wants many things that are good in themselves, such as to eat broccoli or to go on a hiking trip. These, however, one cannot love in the same way as a person is loved, because these are only instruments for the achievement of our own good.

The notion of harmony is naturally associated with happiness, and love, when it is realized perfectly, creates harmony. In Aquinas' opinion, perfect harmony and perfect good (which one can aim at only for its own sake, as an end in itself) is realized only in the person of the Triune God. Paul J. Wadell sums up Aquinas' thinking as follows: "God's happiness is God's very life, and God lives as the everlasting communion of friendship love we call Trinity. For Aquinas, God is not a static entity but the dynamic reality of perfect mutual love. God is the energy of reciprocal love, a communion of persons constituted by the giving and receiving of love. God is that perfect partnership where love offered is love wholly received and wholly returned. God *is* friendship."[7]

To God's friendship belongs the fact that God wants to befriend people, and the character of this friendship is constituted by God's own being: God wants people's love to be similar to God's own being. So God's love is at the same time both a demand and a gift. On the one hand it puts forward quite a high ideal, but at the same time it provides what it demands.

7. Wadell, "Charity," 379.

In other words, God's love cannot be reduced to mere benevolence (*benevolentia*). Genuine love is mutual: a friend is always his friend's friend (*amicus est amico amicus*). The relationship between God and a person is based on this kind of friendship. A problem in the connection between a person and God is also based on this. If the relationship between them is founded on mutual friendship, everything in a person that would make the friendship impossible for God has to be gotten rid of. God can be in relationship only with whoever is his "other self" (*alter ipse*), who rejoices and worries about the same things as he does: this requirement comes out of the definition of friendship. This kind of love is impossible for people to achieve, however. Therefore God includes a person in his love by grace.

Since the love of God as an ideal of love is directed outwards, receiving God's love means showing this attitude toward everybody else. Every single person being equally loved by God, this love gives every person equal value. In Aquinas' opinion a person's value is therefore based on the value that God gives to every person, not, for example, on how good, beautiful, or useful the individual is.

However, we have different responsibilities in relationships with different people. Children and parents have a certain relationship with each other, which is different from the relationship between spouses, for example. In a way we have to love those who are close to use "more." Although this leads to a certain inequality, without it our social system would collapse, which in practice would mean that our love would have failed. Nevertheless, it does not follow from the fact that I love my spouse in a different way from my employer that one of them has more value than the other.

In the same way, we can simultaneously love a person but hate what he does. For example, we can love a criminal without accepting his grievous and unjust acts. As was stated above, love primarily means that, as far as I am able, I act for the best of another. I must therefore act for the best of, for example, a criminal, or my enemy, although I do not accept their actions, words, or convictions. Loving an enemy primarily means loving someone else because he is equally loved by God. Thus I do not love him *because* he is my enemy, for that way I would have to love something that I, by definition, cannot love. According to Aquinas, loving one's enemy also has the benefit of preventing us from becoming bitter and developing the wrong kind of anger toward them.

QUESTIONS FOR CONSIDERATION

1. Give examples of temperance in various spheres of life.

2. "Having faith means that you do not know." Discuss.

3. Does the virtue of love require that you have loving feelings?

4. Think of examples of wisdom. How would you imitate them?

4

APPLICATIONS OF VIRTUES

A VIRTUE IS A disposition that guides practice. In order to understand the meaning of virtues, it helps to examine some concrete areas of human life in which there have been recent attempts to benefit from virtues. In this chapter I will survey virtue ethics, virtue epistemology, positive psychology, and the use of virtues in politics. Previous chapters have hopefully provided the reader with an idea of the overall role of virtue in human life.

VIRTUES AND ETHICS

After the Second World War, Western ethical theory entered a crisis. When initially well-meaning ideologies such as Communism and Fascism ended up resorting to extremely violent practices, it became more difficult than before to believe that we can somehow take for granted that people are able to understand right and wrong. The public role of religion as a moral guarantor gradually started to weaken, especially after the 1960s. Although people's innate religiosity did not disappear, religion and morality started to live their own lives separate from each other, and other institutions that had had a moral-pedagogical function no longer saw themselves as moral guardians.

At the same time, in philosophical and natural scientific circles, critical voices started to be heard regarding human, or other beings', inherent teleology or determinism. According to various theories of natural law, it was the essence of every being that ultimately determined what was good for each being. But if this essence did not exist, then this theory about the essence of beings could not be used as a general, universally binding moral foundation. Behind the rise of virtue theory, a general anti-theoretical movement can be seen in the philosophy of science (such as, for example, Paul Feyerabend's methodological anarchism) and the rise of communitarism in political philosophy. By some estimations, the rise of virtue ethics correlates with postmodern individualism.[1]

Two theories, utilitarianism and deontology, were looked to for help in answering the problems mentioned above regarding the bases for ethics. According to utilitarianism, the key measure of a moral act is whether it produces the greatest amount of good for the greatest number of people. According to deontology, reason gives us universally valid principles that everyone should observe in all situations. The goodness of an act is not defined by its consequences, but goodness is a characteristic of the commandment itself. Sometimes it is said that virtues have completely fallen off the agenda of Western philosophy since the Middle Ages, but this does not hold true. For example, Kant's works contain a lot of theorizing about

1. For a detailed account of virtue ethics, see Statman, *Virtue Ethics*. Russell, *Cambridge Companion to Virtue Ethics*.

virtues. Similarly, the thought of responsibility is not only an idea that came in with Christianity but is present as early pre-Christian times, for example in Cicero.

In her essay "Modern Moral Philosophy" (1958), the influential Oxford moral philosopher Elisabeth Anscombe put her finger on the weak points of the theories just mentioned, and this essay is generally considered the start of modern virtue ethics, or theorizing about virtue overall. The problems of deontology and utilitarianism, long known about, were behind Anscombe's critique. If a giver of law does not exist, what are the responsibilities really based on? Why should welfare be the key factor in ethical reflection? The events of the Second World War mentioned above had affected the belief in people's ability to, by reasoning (separate from other mental faculties such as empathy and emotions in general), find right ways of acting. In academic moral philosophy circles, energy was concentrated mainly on thinking about the meaning of moral concepts. Anscombe's colleague, Alasdair MacIntyre, described Western culture as being in a state in which moral concepts (such as "right," "wrong," "responsibility") were still being used without anyone knowing what they mean or what they are based on.[2]

Since then, virtue ethicists have criticized utilitarians and deontologists with several other arguments. For example, is it really true that a right act is the kind that is done by following rules and in which the agent is able to present her theory in a coherent package? Virtue ethicists have noted that the problem of traditional ethical theories has been their vagueness. Since rules have had to be created to fit ever-changing situations, they have become so vague and general that they hardly have any use. A consequence has also been the practical note that ethicists

2. See MacIntyre, *After Virtue?*.

familiar with theory do not appear to have any particular wisdom in comparison to those who make decisions, such as doctors, soldiers, police, and parents. In addition, a focus on rules fundamentally distorts our moral landscape. For example, it is possible for a person not to break any rule or responsibility but nevertheless act inhumanely; or similarly a person can act within his rights and be cruel. In the same way, it is problematic if we think that we can do whatever we want as long as we do not violate someone else's rights, or that we never have good reason to give up or negotiate about some of our rights.

With these kinds of observations, among others, virtue ethicists started to give attention to the fact that there is a deeper level behind moral rules and responsibilities: the characteristics of the person who is acting, in other words, *character*. In short, according to virtue ethics the rightness of an action is not a consequence of whether it makes as many as possible happy or whether it expresses a rational principle that can be made universal. (These are good principles in themselves, but insufficient in the opinion of virtue theorists.) Instead, rightness depends on whether the action expresses virtue: in this connection, virtue is a factor that expresses a moral ideal. It is an act that a morally ideal person would do in that situation. In this way, virtue ethics moves the focus away from the act and the driving principle behind it to the agent and his character. The correct and good observance of a rule is not the most fundamental issue, but *how* the rule is observed, what kind of motivational factors it is based on, and what kind of moral person it forms.

So what is, for instance, an empathetic person like? He is highly perceptive of his neighbor's need and gets involved in situations where people have suffered a wrong, he shares their feelings, he wants to change the situation and concretely help them, and by doing so he shows empathy and care with all he is. To put it another way, morality requires a lot more than just doing an act that abides by the rules.

Current virtue ethics contains several different ways to understand the place of virtue in ethical reflection. One way to understand the character of a virtuous act is *eudaimonistic virtue ethics*. Eudaimonistic principles, like happiness, welfare and flourishing, refer to the kind of goal with intrinsic value that every person by nature aims for: we all aim for happiness as a goal in itself. In order for happiness to come about, we need virtues, which are characteristics that make the good life possible. In eudaimonistic virtue ethics, an act is good if it is constitutive with respect to human happiness, in other words if it contributes to something that is naturally good for a person. According to *agent-based virtue ethics*, an act is good if behind it is the kind of character trait we find in morally exemplary individuals.

The ethics of care attempts to broaden ethical consideration beyond principles, rules, and individual virtues to the holistic context in which a person lives and acts. In the ethics of care, the concept of virtue has been of benefit in showing that traditional ethics has concentrated on "masculine" virtues like justice and a sense of responsibility. Instead, "female" virtues, such as helping and caring, have been in the margins, because the voice of women has not been adequately heard. It is not important whether the traits in question are especially masculine or feminine, but rather that thinking about virtue has long drawn from quite an elitist tradition that has historically been the preserve of men. The ethics of care underlines, similar to the way traditional virtue ethics does, the unity of reason and emotions in moral life. In addition, it pays attention to the broader context of the moral life, such as power and dependence in relationships. According to Carol Gilligan, a key theoretician of the ethics of care, ethics that bases itself on justice concentrates on universal rights, impersonal procedures, and formal responsibilities, whereas the ethics of care is interested in responsibility, narratives, empathy, and people's individual needs.[3] These two approaches should not, however, be seen as competing against each other but as mutually complementary. Virtue-ethical thinking has also influenced epistemology in many different ways. One example of this is Miranda Fricker's theory of "epistemic injustice," by which she means different ways of excluding unwanted persons and perspectives from public discussion.[4]

Amongst virtue ethicists there are different understandings of what, in the end, the relationship is between the rule and the character of the agent. Supporters of the *weaker* theory (such as Aristotle and Thomas Aquinas) are of the opinion that some actions are wrong regardless of who does them and what his intentions are. For example, Aristotle says that adultery is always wrong regardless of when it is committed, who with, and from what motive. Supporters of the *stronger* theory (such as Anscombe and MacIntyre) think that, insofar as ethical and metaphysical naturalism is accepted, the only coherent way is to reduce moral concepts to characteristics of the person, in which case the independent area delineated by the weaker theory disappears. Supporters of the stronger theory could say, with Aristotle, that adultery is always wrong, but the basis for this would not be that the act is always wrong in itself; rather, an exemplary virtuous person would never do it.

Virtue ethics makes ethical theorizing messier, but virtue ethicists consider this to be essentially a good thing. Rule theories often require that actions and choices can

3. Gilligan, *In a Different Voice.*
4. Fricker, *Epistemic Injustice.*

be easily divided into two baskets, right and wrong. Taking virtues into account, reality is much more complicated. Recognition of this truth helps in better understanding the various values that people try to adopt and balance in their own lives.

In MacIntyre's lifework on virtues, one of his main goals has been to show how virtues are tied up with different cultures and traditions. Later, I will return to the question of whether this places relativism at the core of virtue theory. We can, however, consider as a positive aspect the heuristic remark that helps us to understand the divergence between different cultures regarding ethical reflection. Accordingly some differences of opinion in ethics are understandable (although not necessarily solvable), because they are the products of different traditions. Seen from a global perspective, people's action is, in reality, not driven by some principle that can be applied universally, but by their tradition.

If concrete life is most central to ethics, not abstract rules, this also changes what we consider to be the most important ethical source material. Virtue ethicists diligently use literature and real people as moral examples whose actions make some virtue or vice concrete. Virtue-ethical thinking is naturally associated with modern moral psychology, which, for example, studies how a certain kind of morally exemplary behavior inspires people and how moral reflection and choices happen in practice.

Naturally, virtue ethics has received several kinds of criticism. In what follows I will briefly present the main points of criticism and how they have been responded to.[5]

What justifies actions? In normative ethics, a fundamental question is, On what basis is an action good?

5. In a more detail, see Statman, *Virtue Ethics*, 18–25; Hursthouse, "Virtue Ethics"; Athanassoulis, "Virtue Ethics."

Traditional theories have a clear answer to this. Virtue theory however seems plagued with a collection of problems. Some ethicists say that an act is good if it increases happiness. But it is quite possible for an immoral person to be happy and satisfied with his life. Why should he become virtuous? However, the same problem plagues traditional theories: Why should I obey that particular command or think of others' best? And what about Hume's guillotine? (One cannot conclude from how things are, how they should be.) To put it another way, normative ethical principles cannot be derived from empirical data. It is a different matter to present a judgment based on data, according to which a certain type of behavior B increases positive feelings and experiences of happiness, than it is to claim that B is morally right. For example, the following three statements do not mean the same thing:

a. Bill hit Bob and Bob got hurt. (A judgment concerning Bob's welfare.)

b. Bill did wrong in hitting Bob. (A judgment concerning the justification for Bill's action.)

c. People may not hit each other. (A normative recommendation of action.)

It is in principle possible for virtue ethicists to hold to Hume's guillotine but nevertheless express objective judgments about some models of behavior. By observing human life, it is justifiable to make a judgment that hitting does not typically serve anyone's welfare. The judgment can be a normative judgment (b) without being a normative prescription or guide for action (c).

The problem of applicability. Those who favor traditional theories of knowledge have been eager to point out that virtue epistemology is not able to give clear and concrete guidance for action. In virtue theorists' view this is not a real problem. First, the same kind of problem affects traditional theories. Second, virtue theories do give guidance for action, but they are not of the character that traditional theories would suggest (carry out action X because rule Y recommends that you do it). Rather, virtue-ethical guidance for action is as follows: "carry out an action that expresses gentleness, justice, and moderation," or "carry out an action that a morally ideal person would do." In addition, virtue ethicists note that it is morally problematic to provide straightforward guidance for problems that are extremely complex in character.

Self-centeredness. If rule or duty is not at the core of the analysis, does it not mean that virtue ethics is basically self-centered, because it focuses precisely on the agent's ethical action and development into a better person? However, acting out of mere self-interest would be a failure from the viewpoint of virtue theories. Virtue is essentially about finding the best for someone else and even sacrificing oneself for another's good. A person who thinks only about himself cannot be virtuous.

Moral luck. The attainment of virtue appears to be radically dependent on luck. If you are born into a virtuous community, you will more easily become virtuous than if you are born into a community characterized by vice. The response to this critique has been to admit it. It really is the case that human life is delicate in this way. This is not seen as undermining virtue theories, however, but rather confirming them. Happiness and welfare are delicate and therefore protecting them is so important and requires great effort.

Cultural relativism. A particular, named virtue can mean completely different things in different cultures. A good example of this is magnanimity. In classical philosophy magnanimity was a key quality of a good person but later it was considered a vice. However, cultural differences are not all that great. In no culture is it thought that loyalty is a vice or that cowardice is a virtue. In practice, the differences often concern the way in which an action displays virtue or vice. But here we already share a lot of common ground, including a common moral vocabulary.

Conflict between virtues. Is it not in principle possible that an individual's or community's virtues lead to a contradictory situation in which one virtue suggests one way of acting and another virtue suggests a different way? Once again it has to be said that the same kind of stalemate can in principle also come about in all ethical systems. Different models of virtue ethics contain inherent hierarchies and they present a certain hierarchy of values and virtues. One way to approach this challenge is to emphasize the unity of virtues, which is a part of Aristotelian virtue theory: virtues require and support each other in different ways. Instead of thinking about a hierarchy of virtues, one's action should be directed toward realizing as many different virtues as possible.[6]

Situationism. As already stated, situationism challenges the classical concept of virtue, according to which a person has stable and deeply rooted character traits that are expressed consistently. If there are no such traits, it is somewhat pointless to talk about developing them or living according to them. However, situationism does not pose a major challenge to virtue theories. For example, Kristjánsson presents his own estimation that, from the viewpoint of psychologists, it does not make sense to conduct the context-versus-character discussion from absolutely fixed positions. Actually, everyone admits that both influence a person's action, and the only differences are in the degree to which each influences the agent. Some philosophers

6. On the conflict of virtues, see McInerny, *The Difficult Good.*

nevertheless seem to continue to hold to an either/or type of viewpoint, which according to Kristjánsson does not take account of the discussion or empirical data.[7]

Does virtue ethics offer anything significantly new compared to traditional theories? Virtue ethicists' criticism of traditional theories is in principle entirely sound, but the same problems nevertheless seem also to affect virtue ethics itself. In a sense all theories are in the same boat if we assess them according to whether they give us a means of solving ethical problems easily, self-evidently, and in a way pleasing to everyone. The most significant new thing and advantage that virtue ethics brings is a challenge to the simplistic presuppositions that have been written into traditional theories. By increasing the number of factors in the equation, virtue ethics makes ethical reflection more difficult, but at the same time it is more faithful to the experience of the human subject when he or she is making ethical choices and searching for the good life.

VIRTUES AND KNOWLEDGE

In recent epistemology, the old definition of knowledge, according to which knowledge is justified true belief, has turned out to be problematic in many ways. It is possible to find ourselves in situations in which this definition is met but we nevertheless do not have genuine knowledge. This can happen if our knowledge is based, for example, on a lucky coincidence (these situations are called Gettier events).

The character of Gettier events is as follows. Imagine that you are driving across the US and you get to the countryside in which there are beautiful barns all around. You immediately form the belief that: "There is a beautiful barn

7. See Kristjánsson, *Virtues and Vices.*

in that field." However, unknown to you, you have arrived in a region called Fake Barn County. The name comes from the fact that, in that region, empty barn structures have been put up in the fields for the benefit of tourists. It so happens, though, that the barn that you are looking at right at that moment is the only genuine barn in the whole county. Thus you now have a justified true belief, but no knowledge. Why? Because your belief is dependent on luck. In Gettier events luck comes into the picture twice. First, you have bad luck in the form of ignorance. You have never heard of cunning farmers who build fake barns. Then good luck follows this bad luck: the only genuine barn happens to be in front of your eyes at that moment.

Virtue theories attempt to respond to Gettier events by moving the emphasis of the analysis to the way in which we acquire knowledge. The fact that our knowledge accords with a definition is not the most important thing. Instead, genuine knowledge is based on a reliable process carried out by a reliable, intellectually virtuous person.

Intellectual virtue is, roughly defined, the kind of action that can be expected from an ideal acquirer of knowledge. Such qualities as carefulness, openness, critical awareness, independence, courage, humility, fortitude, and honesty have been suggested as intellectual virtues. The following have often been classified as intellectual vices: carelessness, obstinacy, being uncritical, dishonesty, cowardice, inability to receive feedback, blindness to one's own mistakes, a narrow sphere of interest, and so on.

In classical texts and texts from the Middle Ages, attention was given to virtue in different ways. Aristotle's definition of knowledge was based on virtues that ensured that an observation was true. These kinds of virtues were, for example, sight, intuition, and memory. A little later, the meaning of virtue broadened to include a person's whole character. In the Middle Ages, Thomas Aquinas, for example, suggested a complicated definition of knowledge that placed Aristotle's earlier remarks into a broader and more comprehensive context. The acquisition of knowledge required habituation and the exercise of many kinds of virtuous character traits.

In Aristotelian virtue theory, practical wisdom is a primary virtue that regulates all other virtues. A person cannot have real moral or intellectual virtues without practical wisdom. After the Enlightenment the focus gradually started to shift from the knower and her characteristics to the knower's beliefs and their characteristics. By the time we reach the mid-twentieth century, virtues are almost completely absent from ethics and epistemology. A significant factor in the change was the essay on moral philosophy by Elisabeth Anscombe, mentioned earlier. However, it took twenty years before Anscombe's thoughts started to be applied in epistemology. In 1980, Ernest Sosa published a pivotal article, "The Raft and the Pyramid," in which he criticized the two dominant and competing models of epistemology, fundamentalism and coherentism. According to coherentism (the raft), our beliefs are justified if they are compatible with our other beliefs. The problem of coherentism, according to Sosa, is, however, that it cannot offer ways to understand situations in which, for example, we have beliefs that are based on observations and that are in contradiction with our other beliefs. Furthermore, it is possible for us to have a coherent system that nevertheless does not correspond to how things are in reality. Therefore mere coherence is insufficient to justify our beliefs.

According to the model of epistemology known as fundamentalism (the pyramid), our beliefs are justified if they are basic beliefs or are based on basic beliefs that have come about, for example, on the basis of observations. The problem of fundamentalism concerns whether it can offer some kind of common denominator to the various fundamentalist principles without the bottom of the pyramid constantly being dug deeper. By attempting to justify the existence of basic beliefs, fundamentalism threatens to sink into eternal regression.

Sosa suggests that virtues can help us to move out of this dilemma. By virtue, Sosa means an innate or acquired ability that reliably helps us to gain the truth. According to this definition, knowledge is true belief that comes about when intellectual virtues are exercised. The shift away from analysis of the characteristics of beliefs to the characteristics of the analyzer is apparent in Sosa's proposals. This change in perspective helps to solve the problems that affected earlier models. An agent-centered perspective combines different ways of justification and variations in the body of evidence. Coherence can also be considered a virtue.

The feminist philosopher Lorraine Code tries to take Sosa's idea even further.[8] According to Code, it is not enough for epistemology to remain at the level of abilities; attention should also be paid more widely to a person's actions. Epistemic responsibility is of key importance in knowing, and this guides the operation of all abilities and other virtues. This is the case because the agent acquiring knowledge is active. If it was just a question of passive observation, the reliable operation of the senses and other abilities would be sufficient. Most knowledge, however, requires more complex processing, at which time it is essential that this kind of activity is reliable. Code also notes how the acquisition of knowledge and its evaluation are in various ways dependent on social context and history. This naturally makes epistemology messier. Instead of epistemology trying to

8. Code, *Epistemic Responsibility.*

offer universal definitions, it should focus more attention on the complexity of human existence.

In current epistemology, the discussion that Sosa and Code started is apparent in the form of two different types of basic theory. According to "virtue reliabilists," virtues are a matter of abilities, whereas "virtue responsibilists" emphasize the significance of the whole personality. This division is sometimes expressed by talking about faculty virtues and character/trait virtues. Typical faculty virtues are, for example, sharp eyesight and a good memory, whereas character/trait virtues include carefulness, courage, perseverance, and open-mindedness, for example. However, there is no reason to draw a precise distinction between different types of virtue. Many faculty virtues require character/trait virtues to function perfectly. Sharp eyesight is of no benefit if, at the same time, you are lazy and careless, and, on the other hand, many character/trait virtues are in practice realized via various abilities.

The discussion between reliabilists and responsibilists nevertheless highlights the different tasks that epistemology and especially virtue epistemology, are seen to have. Jason Baehr has classified virtue epistemologies into four different groups by which the different ways of using virtue theory become clearly understandable.[9]

The varieties of virtue epistemology can be analyzed by comparing them to the ways in which epistemology has earlier been practiced. *Traditional* epistemology is interested in themes such as scepticism, the definition of knowledge, and intellectual justification, and some virtue epistemologies continue to address these questions with the help of virtues. *Autonomous* virtue epistemology is the name given to models that see virtues as objects of

9. Baehr, *The Inquiring Mind*, 191–205.

philosophical analysis and emphasize in different ways how the traditional viewpoint could be broadened.

First, according to so-called *strong traditional virtue epistemology*, virtues provide a solution to the problems of traditional epistemology, such as Gettier events. A typical representative of this line of thought is Linda Zagzebski.[10] In her opinion virtues should be at the center of traditional epistemology and, thereby, a fundamental and necessary part of the definition of knowledge. Zagzebski's virtue epistemology is made up of two components. First, knowledge should be motivated by intellectual virtue and, second, it should be based on the kind of virtuous action that reliably generates true answers. These demands are excessive, however. In most situations we can have knowledge without being motivated in the right way. I can, for example, form the, in itself, correct belief that "the mayor is standing in Times Square" without being a bit interested in where the mayor is or who is standing in Times Square. Moreover, Zagzebski's theory does not cover Gettier events in which the person mistakenly believes *p*, even though he is acting virtuously while believing *p*. We can be in a situation where, despite stretching our abilities and virtues to their limits, it is impossible for us to form true beliefs. Many theories that were, in the past, generally accepted and considered scientific, but eventually turned out to be mistaken, are examples of such cases.

According to *weak traditional virtue epistemology*, virtues offer, at most, support for traditional epistemology but they do not actually revolutionize anything regarding how the problem of knowledge has been traditionally dealt with. Representatives of this line of thought are, among others, Ernest Sosa, Duncan Pritchard, John Greco, and Jason Baehr. The role of virtues is thus to confirm the traditional

10. Zagzebski, *Virtues of the Mind*.

definition of knowledge. For example, Duncan Pritchard presents the following definition, which, in his opinion, is able to withstand most of the challenges to the definition of knowledge.

> S knows that p if and only if (i) S's true belief that p is produced by a reliable cognitive character trait so that his cognitive success is dependent in a fundamental way on his own cognitive action and (ii) S's belief that p is safe.[11]

Support for Pritchard's definition comes not just from virtues (which according to him can be understood as either faculty virtues or character/trait virtues) but also from the so-called safety principle. By this principle, there cannot be a kind of possible world that is similar to the actual world but in which a belief is untrue. In other words, according to the safety principle a person should not, in believing p, be easily wrong.

According to *strong autonomic virtue epistemology*, the problems of modern epistemology are so deep that traditional thinking should be abandoned or at least radically modified on the basis of virtues. For example, the definition of the concept of knowledge is, from this angle, quite futile and hopeless. Instead, much more interesting questions include: How can we develop into ideal knowers? How can we assess the merits of different intellectual communities?

According to Jonathan Kvanvig, an advocate of the strong thesis, epistemology should present the kind of description of cognitive action that is faithful to our cognitive experience and that helps us to understand how to maximize our potential to find truth and avoid error.[12] The basic criticism of the strong thesis is the following. Although, for

11. Pritchard, *Knowledge*, 74.

12. Kvanvig, *The Intellectual Virtues*; *The Value of Knowledge*.

example, analysis of the concept of knowledge can be very dry, it does not mean that it is useless practically. And even if we would like to maximize the usefulness of epistemology, it does not follow from this that analysis aiming for conceptual clarity, for instance, is useless, even though it benefits only a few (those who are able to understand the discourse in question).

If Kvanvig's thesis is left out of the radical criticism of traditional epistemology, it mellows into *weak autonomic virtue epistemology*. In this case, virtues are seen as interesting and useful but without the recommendation of radical change. Virtues bring both a complementary addition to traditional epistemology and a number of distinctive questions that are genuinely epistemic but that are genuinely different from the questions that traditional epistemology addresses. Lorraine Code, Robert Roberts, and William Wood are typical representatives of this position.

There are many relevant questions that fit the above-mentioned description. Baehr divides these into five categories. First, we can examine the relation between intellectual virtue and other abilities. What is the relationship between moral and intellectual virtues? How are abilities, virtues, and other character traits, such as temperament, linked? Second, we can examine what makes an ability or characteristic into an intellectual virtue. Is it a question of its effectiveness or reliability in discovering the truth? Third, it is possible to examine virtues from the perspective of the philosophy of psychology. Are some cognitive states required for virtuous knowing? What does "the love of knowledge" actually mean? Fourth, we can take an individual virtue or vice as an object of investigation. What is, for example, the meaning of wisdom or open-mindedness? Fifth, we can investigate the various applications of virtues (applied virtue epistemology). What does successful acquisition and analysis of knowledge require in a certain context (such as journalism, law, or theology)? Can and may virtues be taught?

The cross-section given above of different manifestations of virtue epistemology shows what a broad phenomenon it is. However, despite many differences between them, the various virtue epistemologies have basic features in common. First, virtue epistemologies are by nature normative and thus the opposite of, for example, Quine's suggestion of naturalizing epistemology in such a way that it would address only non-normative aspects connected with knowledge.

Second, in virtue epistemology, knowledge is understood as coming about by the influence of intellectual virtue. In other words, virtue must be a central part of the causal chain that produces knowledge for us. In Gettier events, belief comes about by chance, which removes the status of knowledge from belief. According to virtue epistemology, knowledge requires a person's successful use of their cognitive abilities. This means that, in believing that p, S can be considered worthy, because his correctly functioning cognitive abilities are an essential factor in the formation of the belief. A causal dependence of knowledge from virtues distinguishes the genuine knowledge from Gettier events, where a person also uses their cognitive abilities, but in these events intellectual ability or virtue is not a fundamental factor in the formation of knowledge.[13]

In current epistemology there are several other important discussions that have caused philosophers to think about virtues. One discussion concerns the role of trust and testimonies in knowing. John Hardwig has remarked that we are obliged to accept that we are intellectually dependent on each other.[14] In other words, it is possible for

13. Greco, *Achieving Knowledge*, 12, 71–90.

14. Hardwig, "Epistemic Dependence"; "The Role of Trust in

us to form a belief independently of others only in rare, exceptional cases. Therefore the Enlightenment demand for intellectual autonomy is very problematic. One cannot trust just anybody, though. One way to proceed in these situations is to evaluate the provider of evidence in terms of intellectual virtues. Do his earlier actions display care and evenhandedness, or intellectual vices such as dishonesty and an uncritical approach? Similarly, if I have no direct access to either the actual evidence or knowledge about the provider of the testimony as an intellectual agent, withholding an expression of opinion is the intellectually virtuous course of action.

Miranda Fricker has applied virtue epistemology from the perspective of various intellectual vices.[15] According to Fricker, there is such a thing as epistemic injustice, which is evident in both testimonial and hermeneutical form. Testimonial injustice blocks some individuals or groups from acquiring knowledge. This blocking can appear as, for example, underestimation, deliberate misinterpretation, or silencing, which arise from various types of prejudices, for instance. Fricker uses as an example cases in which Afro-Americans were not treated as reliable witnesses in US court sessions. Hermeneutical injustice is in question when an assumption or prejudice prevents the listener from understanding or from taking seriously what the other person says. As an antidote, Fricker recommends testimonial sensitivity, which comprises intellectual virtues such as open-mindedness and wisdom.

Handling these kinds of themes, for example, broadens the scope of philosophy, in this case especially of epistemology, and brings it closer to both everyday reality and the forms of classical philosophy that understand

Knowledge."

15. Fricker, *Epistemic Injustice.*

philosophy expressly as a life-management skill. Some virtue epistemologists follow this line of thought but others remain within an established analytical tradition. However, we have no particular reason to consider these as mutually exclusive projects.

VIRTUES AND POSITIVE PSYCHOLOGY

The basic approach of psychology toward human life has long been problem-oriented: the job of psychology is to address various problems connected with mental functioning. This starting point has defined the emphases of research, with the result that we have a lot of knowledge about various mental disturbances but do not know much at all about how we can promote welfare. *Positive psychology* attempts to broaden the approach, so that more attention in psychology would be given to factors that increase people's welfare. Today, psychologist Martin Seligman is the leading voice in positive psychology.

In short, positive psychology investigates the processes and factors that promote the flourishing of individuals, communities, and institutions, and that further holistic wellbeing and optimal ability to function. Naturally, positive psychology widely exploits the discussion about virtues; as in the eudaimonistic tradition, virtues are seen as necessary for wellbeing. In particular, positive psychology examines three areas considered fundamental with respect to wellbeing:

a. Positive experiences

b. Positive character traits

c. Positive institutions

Virtues are especially associated with points b and c. Positive character traits are approached from the perspective of virtues. Positive institutions are understood as structures that support virtuous activity and the development of a virtuous personality. These are, for example, democracy and open decision-making processes, an unbroken family, satisfying friendships, and epistemic practices of a kind that reflect intellectual virtues.

Positive psychology has received critique from many different sides. Many "traditional" psychologists have not particularly liked the negative label placed on them. Philosophers specializing in Aristotle have not been satisfied with the occasionally superficial way in which the Philosopher's texts have been used in positive psychology circles. Moreover, the methods used by the movement (and especially some spin-off projects) have been criticized as being superficial, and the movement has been seen as having cultish characteristics and being simplistic.

In this chapter I will talk about the critical discussion surrounding positive psychology. I will concentrate especially on the following questions: How can happiness be measured? Is positive psychology science or a sermon on morals? Is positive psychology right-wing thinking dressed up as science? Does situationism pull the mat from underneath positive psychology?

At the center of Aristotelian virtue theory is the concept of *eudaimonia*, and positive psychology takes this as its starting point. Happiness appears to be that which, in the end, people aim for and value. Positive experiences, and structures and institutions that reflect positivity, support subjective happiness, and happiness for its part increases positive experiences.

But how can happiness be measured? There are three main lines of thought on this among psychologists: the hedonistic, the satisfaction, and the eudaimonistic theories.[16]

16. Kristjansson, *Virtues and Vices*, 33–65.

According to hedonistic theory, the best guarantee of happiness is simply the feeling of subjective happiness and pleasure. Notice that in this connection, hedonism does not mean unrestrained, lecherous behavior but that an individual feels that there are more causes of pleasure than displeasure in her life. If this is the case, a person is happy.

There are several difficult problems associated with hedonistic happiness theory. First, imagine that you could be plugged into the computer from the *Matrix* movie that creates the illusion in your mind that you are living an easy and rich live. In that movie a character called Cypher decides he wants to be plugged back into the illusion machine and escape from his detestable life in a stuffy cave. Only a few people would be willing to say, however, that Cypher's life in the illusion machine would really be happy. In any case, Cypher expresses to the operators of the machine, the "agents," his wish that he could live a life in which he was rich and famous.

Second, another problem connected with hedonistic theory is that a person becomes used to his level of happiness quite quickly. When certain basics are in order, a person's subjective happiness will not increase even if he gained all the money and glory in the world. Therefore it is quite possible that Bill Gates and the person next door are both equally subjectively happy despite the difference in wealth between them.

Third, hedonism in its simplest form does not make it possible to distinguish between different types of pleasures. For example, delighting over other people's misfortunes or teasing the girl in front of you by pulling her hair is a source of pleasure and as such is good enough for someone as the content of a good life. It is, however, difficult to think that someone being empowered through delight over other people's misfortunes would be genuinely happier than, for example, a person who derives happiness from being a volunteer at the Red Cross.

According to satisfaction theory, happiness is best assessed according to the individual's own subjective estimate, which relates to one's life as a whole and especially to one's achievements. In this way it is possible to say that, for example, Jay Gatsby, the main character in F. Scott Fitzgerald's *The Great Gatsby*, is not happy, despite being rich and famous, because he does not have as his own the woman he loves. Though he has had many positive experiences in life, he is nevertheless unhappy. In the same way it is possible to say that someone who has experienced great adversity but has gained something deep, is happy.

The problems of satisfaction theory concern a person's ability to explain and interpret events in a positive way. In addition, it is natural for us to forget negative experiences and highlight the positive ones. We often organize our lives in the form of stories, but we are quite unreliable tellers of our own life story. We exaggerate or play down matters according to whether they suit the story we like at that moment. Our story can often be based on pure self-deception. It is also not unusual for us to radically change our story during our lifetime: experiences that we at one time considered negative can become positive, and vice versa.

According to eudaimonistic theory, the subjective theories just described are not completely reliable measures of happiness. We have to trust objective criteria instead. Consequently, we estimate a person's happiness in terms of those factors we know genuinely to increase happiness. These are, for example, physical and mental health, networks of friends, positive feelings, succeeding in life and the opportunity to express oneself in different ways, succeeding in moral and intellectual virtues, and so on.

The individual factors mentioned in these kinds of lists are neither necessary nor sufficient for happiness. We know that a very sick person can be very happy and that mere health is not necessarily enough for happiness. We can nevertheless say that a person is more likely to be happy if he has several of the things on this list than if he does not have them. It seems that the factors on the lists of eudaimonistic theories are those that, at best, make happiness *possible* but do not guarantee it.

In the end, does eudaimonistic theory make the measurement of happiness possible, though? It would feel strange to say to someone who has several of the items mentioned on the list (or even all of them), but was nevertheless unhappy, that "yes, objectively measured, you are happy, even though it does not feel like it." It seems, then, that we should somehow take account of the subjective estimation of an individual's own experience of happiness. This is not very easy, though, precisely because of the problems presented in connection with subjective theories.

As a solution, Seligman has suggested the sum of five factors. These factors are: positive feelings, participation, significance, positive relationships, and achievements. Of these, the first is purely subjective and the others contain subjective elements although they can be assessed with objective criteria. Participation and relationships are particularly connected with virtues. Participation that displays virtues, such as in the form of helping someone, increases wellbeing. In the same way, if relationships are realized in a way described by virtues, life in principle meets the requirements to be satisfying.

For positive psychology it is essential that something is objectively measurable because it aims toward the creation of concrete practices and structures that further wellbeing and happiness. However, no matter how much we increase the number of various measures and criteria, it is unlikely that we will ever achieve a perfect and robust means of measuring happiness objectively. Our knowledge of the actual level of happiness will always remain more or less an approximation.

In addition to the fact that objective criteria are still very difficult to come by, this move toward objectivity has raised a new concern. Is it now the case that positive psychology offers a normative formula for what a good life is? Seligman and his colleagues have tried to avoid giving this impression, but the matter is still somewhat unresolved. However, empirical evidence collected from different cultures and religions supports the conclusion that moral and intellectual virtues strongly correlate with wellbeing, and people themselves consider virtues to be key requirements for wellbeing.

A key philosophical critique surrounds situationism, which we looked at earlier. Although the philosophical debate about situationism is still going on, in psychological circles it died down some time ago. The current consensus accepts that both personality and environment influence behavior. Naturally, different researchers emphasize either personality or environment in different ways, but these are not seen as mutually exclusive factors. In its own vision, positive psychology highlights how we can create the kinds of structures that support virtuous action.

The theme of wellbeing also relates to political realities. Is talk of virtues and positivity just veiled right-wing ideology in which the individual's job is to climb out of a hole on his own—a hole that unjust structures have pushed him into? This critique is called the individualist bias of positive psychology. Positive psychologists have typically evaded the accusation by stating that what is in question is a kind of chicken-and-egg problem. We do not really know where the core of the problem lies, but pragmatically we should start from the individual, ourselves, instead of first attempting to change complex institutions.

Kristjánsson says, for example, that the available empirical material more strongly supports a perspective starting out from the individual, in which there is recognition that community wellbeing and functioning depend on individuals and their attitudes and abilities.[17] First, logically, political virtue requires moral virtue; we do not know what a just state is like if we have no idea of what a just person is like. Second, psychologically, we know that a person's, especially a child's, moral development happens under the influence of her immediate surroundings, the influence of family and friends, and surrounding institutions have only a secondary influence.

VIRTUES AND POLITICS

Does the purpose justify the means? Does a politician benefit from being virtuous? In this chapter I will examine different perspectives on how the role of virtues has been understood in politics. I start with Niccolo Machiavelli's cynical viewpoint, from which we will progress toward a slightly more hopeful model.

An unusually open and direct answer is presented in Niccolo Machiavelli's *The Prince*, which is one of the classics of political philosophy: according to Machiavelli, a pliant moral backbone and outward pretence at virtue aid a politician in his rule. Machiavelli teaches:

> And you have to understand this, that a prince, especially a new one, cannot observe all those things for which men are esteemed, being often forced, in order to maintain the state, to act

17. Kristjanssón, *Virtues and Vices*, 64–65.

contrary to faith, friendship, humanity, and religion. Therefore it is necessary for him to have
a mind ready to turn itself accordingly as the
winds and variations of fortune force it, yet, as I
have said above, not to diverge from the good if
he can avoid doing so, but, if compelled, then to
know how to set about it.[18]

According to Machiavelli, the good governor must do
his all to appear as the embodiment of the virtues. However, the reality, and what the governor does, are two different things. In his book, Machiavelli refers to an unnamed
governor who preaches about peace and loyalty but who
is actually an enemy of these virtues. This moral duplicity
has nevertheless made him into a successful governor. In
Machiavelli's view, even the people often know that they are
lied to and understand the way that the governor distorts
virtues. However, if the governor is caught red-handed
doing something deceptive, he must explain that he did it
with the people's best interest in mind. The interpretation
of Machiavelli's writings is not straightforward, though. *The
Prince* has been considered a parody and even a veiled critique, not a direct recommendation of a way of acting. The
work can also be read as a neutral description of how affairs
in the world are really managed.

If this is the stark reality, how can we think about
something bigger and better? When talking about the relationship between virtues and politics, it is usual to take as
the starting point Augustine, whose work *The City of God*
has had a significant influence in political philosophy. Many
very different thinkers have constructed their own theories
either as a continuation of Augustine's vision or in criticism
of it. It is not possible here to become acquainted with these
different ways of reading Augustine as a political thinker. In

18. Machiavelli, *The Prince*, XVIII.

what follows I will present some observations that come out of the Augustinian tradition and its basic concepts.

Augustinian virtue politics sees human sin and love as being in tension. On the one hand, a person is fully corrupted by twisted desires. Even in what appear to be the most noble and virtuous acts there is always the hidden seed of selfishness, malevolence, and coveting. This being so, one cannot completely trust a person. It is therefore better for politics to focus only on preventing extremely bad deeds and otherwise to leave people alone with their own opinions. The setting of ideals too high is considered unrealistic.

On the other hand, Augustine recognizes the possibility that in principle any society can establish a state of relative peace. Although this may not necessarily be very long lasting (because of people's sinfulness), it is nevertheless always a good thing worth aiming for. The way to this state of peace is the way of virtues. The more that virtues such as love and justice are realized in society, the better it is for human wellbeing. In *The City of God*, Augustine gives his famous definition of a people: the character of a people is defined according to what and how it loves.

> But if we discard this definition of a people, and, assuming another, say that a people is an assemblage of reasonable beings bound together by a common agreement as to the objects of their love, then, in order to discover the character of any people, we have only to observe what they love. Yet whatever it loves, if only it is an assemblage of reasonable beings and not of beasts, and is bound together by an agreement as to the objects of love, it is reasonably called a people; and it will be a superior people in proportion as

it is bound together by higher interests, inferior
in proportion as it is bound together by lower.[19]

In twentieth-century political philosophy there are
three main lines of thought that draw on Augustinian
teaching on virtue in different ways. According to *Augustinian realism* one cannot expect very great and virtuous
deeds of anyone. Instead, what is important is that the state
reins in expressions of extreme bad while otherwise leaving people more or less alone to have their own opinions.
Reinhold Niebuhr is one of the representatives of this viewpoint. According to *Augustinian liberalism*, it is important
to emphasize justice in particular as a factor in maintaining a democratic society. The most well-known supporter
of liberalism is John Rawls, whose social-contract theory
is expressly based on the virtue of justice. According to
Augustinian civic liberalism, a single virtue is not enough;
rather, flourishing requires a broad range of many virtues.
Martin Luther King Jr. is considered the most well-known
representative of this line.

The relationships between these political models are
very complicated. According to liberalism, realism does not
offer a sufficient basis for a sustainable society. According
to civic liberalism, liberalism offers too little. According to
realism, the other lines of thought set the expectations too
high, and in practice they have to take back their words and
surrender their virtue because the good they represent cannot be made concrete without some kind of compulsion. In
addition, liberalism wants to highlight the carefully defined
virtue of justice, but at the same time it wants to place outside the discussion the tradition or traditions from which
this virtue comes, thereby pulling the mat from under its
own feet. This is the criticism of, for example, Alasdair

19. Augustine, *City of God*, 19:24.

MacIntyre: the dominant concept of justice in the West comes from and is dependent on the Judaeo-Christian tradition, and without a relationship to this tradition the virtue loses its meaningfulness and vitality.

However, those kinds of political models that take one virtue as their guiding principle have been seen to give rise to totalitarian or otherwise violent societies. They have one closely delimited model of the good that is forced on the whole nation. A good example is the virtue of equality in the Communist utopias of the twentieth century.

In a class of its own is criticism of Augustinian politics that holds that virtues do not belong in politics at all. The main critic of Augustinian thought on virtue is Hannah Arendt, who did her doctorate on Augustine's theology of love. Her early thinking and critical stance toward Augustine is evident in her later political philosophy. According to Arendt, love in no way belongs in politics, which should operate only by the criteria of objective justice. For her, love is in practice identical to pathological sentimentalism. A person who loves becomes too intimately involved with the objects of his love, which dims his ability to critically evaluate. Love is, on the one hand, too demanding (and therefore not realistic) and, on the other hand, too partisan and subjective. Good moral philosophy is not necessarily the best political philosophy. Politics has to rise above emotions. Instead, the true political virtue is *respect*. Although I neither can nor should (because nobody can demand it) love everyone and everything, to some extent I can, however, respect others, even my enemies that I can in no way love.

Arendt's concern partly has a basis. However, in her analysis of love, Arendt focuses mainly on distorted forms of love. We all understand that a judge who has fallen in love with the accused will not necessarily act objectively. But a judge who lets a guilty one go free just because he loves her, does not actually act according to love. His perspective is clearly distorted. Although Arendt attempts to sketch out the borderlines of a more just world, it is justifiable to ask whether her critique goes too far.

For example, especially those who hold to feminist ethics of care object to liberalism by noting how the exclusion of aspects such as mutual dependence and vulnerability easily make public discourse quite cold and technocratic. Those who favor the ethics of care have tried to widen our understanding of virtues and have helped us to see better the significance of the unity of virtues.

Martin Luther King Jr. also tried to promote the same kind of balance in his speeches and writings. In one of his speeches he brings up the basic Augustinian concepts of love and power as the object of his analysis and indicates how extreme positions cannot create the necessary balance regarding human wellbeing:

> You see, what happened is that some of our philosophers got off base. And one of the great problems of history is that the concepts of love and power have usually been contrasted as opposites, polar opposites, so that love is identified with a resignation of power, and power with a denial of love. It was this misinterpretation that caused the philosopher Nietzsche, who was a philosopher of the will to power, to reject the Christian concept of love. It was this same misinterpretation which induced Christian theologians to reject Nietzsche's philosophy of the will to power in the name of the Christian idea of love.
>
> Now, we got to get this thing right. What is needed is a realization that power without love is reckless and abusive, and that love without power is sentimental and anemic. Power at

its best is love implementing the demands of justice, and justice at its best is love correcting everything that stands against love. And this is what we must see as we move on.[20]

In the Aristotelian tradition, political virtues have been seen as a natural part of the good life of an individual. An individual can best achieve happiness (for which, virtues are needed) in a community that, in the way it functions, supports the practice of virtues. Philosophers have had varying stances regarding how well a state can teach its citizens virtues. Generally, however, the idea has been treated with suspicion. Even political virtues come about and develop through relationships with those close to us and in small communities. States that try to teach their citizens very clear-cut virtues fall into typical vices. In the words of the Polish philosopher Leszek Kolakowski:

> Socialism as a social or moral philosophy was based on the ideal of human brotherhood, which can never be implemented by institutional means. There has never been, and there will never be, an institutional means of making people brothers. Fraternity under compulsion is the most malignant idea devised in modern times; it is a perfect path to totalitarian tyranny.[21]

Complete anarchy lurks at the other end of the spectrum, of course. A political model in the mid-field tries to avoid the extremes and aims at cultivating the kinds of models of behavior that, on the one hand, make diversity possible but, on the other, prevent society from sliding to the extremes just mentioned. A form of so-called political

20. King, "Where do we go from here?" Quoted in Gregory, *Politics and the Order of Love*, 195.

21. Kolakowski, *Is God Happy?*, 69.

liberalism is currently dominant in the West. An important element in the idea of political liberalism is the thought that in a free society people necessarily have different conceptions of what a good life is, and society must offer everyone the possibility of pursuing what they consider good. The only limit to this pursuit of various goods is that individual goods must not go against the system itself.

Tolerance is sometimes considered a modern key virtue. However, tolerance is quite a complex virtue and it is not present in classical lists of virtues. Naturally, the reason for this is that tolerance can also be a vice. Moreover, what is meant by tolerance can be seen to be included in the virtues of justice and temperance, for example. Instead of elevating one virtue above others in public discourse, it is more natural to try to cultivate a broad group of different virtues. These kinds of virtues are typically called democratic virtues, of which the most typical are the following, for example:

- the practice of civility and respect
- the cultivation of real dialogue by listening and asking questions
- the rejection of appeals to private standards
- the practice of careful moral reasoning
- openness to alternative points of view[22]

In addition, Jeffrey Stout presents the following principles:

- Ability to listen with an open mind
- Temperance to avoid taking and causing offense needlessly

22. See Shields, *Democratic Virtues*, 2.

117

- The practical wisdom to discern the subtleties of a discursive situation
- The courage to speak candidly
- The tact to avoid sanctimonious cant
- The poise to respond to unexpected arguments
- The humility to ask forgiveness from those who have been wronged[23]

It is easy to see how each of the above-mentioned principles can be derived from the four cardinal virtues. These must be seen as principles without which democracy does not remain genuine democracy. At the same time it is clear, however, that not all these principles are always realized everywhere. Practice of these principles requires a trained character.

QUESTIONS FOR CONSIDERATION

1. What can virtues offer to ethical deliberation?
2. How would you cherish intellectual virtues in your own community?
3. What is happiness? Can you want not to be happy?
4. "Virtues have no room in business life, politics and war!" Discuss.

23. Stout, *Democracy and Tradition*, 85.

FINAL WORDS

I HOPE THAT THIS book has given the reader an understanding of what people have been trying to achieve by thinking about virtues and why. Several times is has been clear that being virtuous is difficult, often nearly impossible. So why is it worth talking about virtues at all?

First, virtues set the standard for all of us. We know immediately when we are treated wrongly: *someone else* has not been virtuous. We do not notice our own vice so easily, but the ever-present awareness of what an ideal world would be like gives us an inner desire to strive toward it— although we often fail.

Second, taking virtues into account makes it *more difficult* for us to think and act. The idea of the unity of virtues requires us to be aware of a large number of different factors and to try to balance them against each other. Analysis of our action in terms of virtues prevents us from becoming blinkered, in other words from concentrating on only what is most obvious. Instead, a wide range of good goals lies before us. Often just the realization of how much we lack virtue, of how far we have to go, is a big step in the right direction, whether it be an everyday moral question, something ethically more challenging, or a political debate.

It is best to avoid facile and trivial talk about virtues, though. Human nature being what it is, we can find ourselves trying to whitewash vices with ostensible virtues. Similarly, concentrating only on one or a few virtues and forgetting others ensures that the result is less than desirable. We must not be disappointed when weaknesses and vices are exposed in people we look up to. But it is not worth being cynical. Even though none of us is perfect, some of us display a balanced mix of virtues and therefore serve as good examples. Let us follow them.

BIBLIOGRAPHY

Adams, Robert Merrihew. *A Theory of Virtue: Excellence in Being for the Good*. Oxford: Oxford University Press, 2006.

Alfano, Mark Robert. "The Most Agreeable of All Vices: Nietzsche as Virtue Epistemologist." *British Journal for the History of Philosophy* 21 (2013) 767–90.

Annas, Julia. "The Structure of Virtue." In *Intellectual Virtue: Perspectives from Ethics and Epistemology*, edited by Michael DePaul and Linda Zagzebski, 15–33. Oxford: Oxford University Press, 2003.

Anscombe, Elisabeth. "Modern Moral Philosophy." In *Ethics, Religion and Politics: The Collected Philosophical Papers of G. E. M. Anscombe*, 3:26–42. Minneapolis: University of Minnesota Press, 1981.

Aquinas, Thomas. *Summa Theologica*. http://www.newadvent.org/summa/.

Aristotle. *Nicomachean Ethics*. Translated by J. W. Ross. Oxford: Oxford University Press, 2009.

Athanassoulis, Nafsika. "Virtue Ethics." *Internet Encyclopedia of Philosophy* 2014. http://www.iep.utm.edu/virtue/.

Augustine. *City of God*. Translated by Marcus Dods. New York: Random House, 1999.

Austin, Michael, and Douglas Geivett, eds. *Being Good: Christian Virtues for Everyday Life*. Grand Rapids: Eerdmans, 2012.

Baehr, Jason. *The Inquiring Mind. On Intellectual Virtue and Virtue Epistemology*. Oxford: Oxford University Press, 2011.

Batson, C. Daniel. *The Altruism Question: Toward a Social-Psychological Answer*. Hillsdale: Erlbaum, 1991.

Chesterton, G. K., *Orthodoxy*. London: Catholic Way, 2013.

Bibliography

Code, Lorraine. *Epistemic Responsibility.* Hanover, NH: University Press of New England, 1987.

Cogley, Zac. "A Study of Virtuoes and Vicious Anger." In *Virtues and Their Vices,* edited by Kevin Timpe and Craig A. Boyd, 199–224. Oxford: Oxford University Press, 2014.

Darley, J. M., and C. Daniel Batson. "'From Jerusalem to Jericho': A Study of Situational and Dispositional Variables in Helping Behavior.'" *Journal of Personality an Social Psychology* 27 (1973) 100–108.

DePaul, Michael, and Linda Zagzebski. *Intellectual Virtue: Perspectives from Ethics and Epistemology.* Oxford: Oxford University Press, 2003.

Doris, John. *Lack of Character: Personality and Moral Behavior.* Cambridge: Cambridge University Press, 2002.

Erasmus, Desiderius. *In Praise of Folly.* New York: Penguin, 2004.

Fricker, Miranda. *Epistemic Injustice. Power and the Ethics of Knowing.* Oxford: Oxford University Press, 2007.

Gilligan, Carol. *In a Different Voice: Psychological Theory and Women's Development.* Cambridge: Harvard University Press, 1990.

Greco, John. *Achieving Knowledge: A Virtue-Theoretic Account of Epistemic Normativity.* Oxford: Oxford University Press 2010.

Hardwig, John. "Epistemic Dependence." *The Journal of Philosophy* 82 (1985) 335–49.

———. "The Role of Trust in Knowledge." *The Journal of Philosophy* 88 (1991) 693–708.

Harman, Gilbert. "Moral Philosophy Meets Social Psychology: Virtue Ethics and the Fundamental Attribution Error." *Proceedings of the Aristotelian Society* 99 (1999) 315–31.

Hartshorne, Hugh, and Mark A. May. *Studies in the Nature of Character: Studies in Deceit.* New York: MacMillan, 1928.

Herdt, Jennifer. *Putting on Virtue: The Legacy of Splendid Vices.* Chicago: University of Chicago Press, 2008.

Hogan, Robert. "Much Ado about Nothing: The Person-Situation Debate." *Journal of Research in Personality* 43 (2009) 249.

Hursthouse, Rosalind. "Virtue Ethics." *Stanford Encyclopedia of Philosophy* 2012. http://plato.stanford.edu/entries/ethics-virtue/.

Jost, John T., and Lawrence T. Jost. "Virtue Ethics and the Social Psychology of Character: Philosophical :essons from the Person-Situation Debate." *Journal of Research in Personality* 43 (2009) 253–54.

King, Martin Luther Jr. *"I have a Dream": Writings and Speeches That Changed The World.* New York: HarperCollins, 1992.

Bibliography

Kolakowski, Leszek. *Is God Happy? Selected Essays*. New York: Basic, 2013.

Kristjánsson, Kristján, *Virtues and Vices in Positive Psychology*. Cambridge: Cambridge University Press, 2013

Kvanvig, Jonathan. *The Intellectual Virtues and the Life of the Mind*. Savage, ML: Rowman and Littlefield, 1992.

———. *The Value of Knowledge and the Pursuit of Understanding*. Cambridge: Cambridge University Press 2003.

Lewis, C. S. *The Abolition of Man*. New York: HarperOne, 2015.

Machiavelli, Niccolo. *Prince*. New York: Penguin, 2003.

MacIntyre, Alasdair. *After Virtue*. 3rd ed. South Bend, IN: University of Notre Dame Press, 2007.

Milgram, Stanley. *Obedience to Authority*. New York: Harper & Row, 1974.

———. "Behavioral Study of Obedience." *Journal of Abnormal and Social Psychology* 67 (1963) 371–78.

Miller, Christian B. *Character and Moral Psychology*. Oxford: Oxford University Press, 2014.

———. *Moral Character: An Empirical Theory*. Oxford: Oxford University Press, 2013.

Nietzsche, Friedrich. *Gay Science*. New York: Random House, 1993.

———. *Twilight of the Idols and the Anti-Christ*. New York: Penguin, 1990.

Peterson, Christopher, and Martin Seligman. *Character Strengths and Virtues: A Handbook and Classification*. Oxford: Oxford University Press, 2004.

Pritchard, Duncan. *Knowledge*. London: Palgrave MacMillan, 2009.

Roberts, Robert C., and William J. Wood. *Intellectual Virtues: An Essay in Regulative Epistemology*. Oxford University Press, Oxford 2007.

Rousseau, Jean-Jacques. *Emilé, or on Education*. Translated by Allan Bloom. New York: Basic, 1979.

Russell, Daniel C., ed. *Cambridge Companion to Virtue Ethics*. Cambridge: Cambridge University Press, 2013.

Shields, Jon. *The Democratic Virtues of the Christian Right*. Princeton, NJ: Princeton University Press, 2009.

Sosa, Ernest. "The Raft and the Pyramid: Coherence versus Foundations in the Theory of Knowledge." *Midwest Studies in Philosophy* V (1980) 3–25.

Statman Daniel. *Virtue Ethics: A Critical Reader*. Edinburgh: Edinburgh University Press, 1997.

Timpe, Kevin, and Craig A. Boyd, eds. *Virtues and Their Vices*. Oxford: Oxford University Press, 2014.

Titus, Craig S. "Moral Development and Connecting the Virtues: Aquinas, Porter, and the Flawed Saint." In *Ressourcement Thomism: Sacred Doctrine, the Sacraments, and the Moral Life: Essays in Honor of Romanus Cessario*, edited by Reinhard Hütter and Matthew Levering, 330–52. Washington, DC: Catholic University of America Press, 2010.

Wadell, Paul J. "Charity: How Friendship with God Unfolds in Love for Others." In *Virtues and Their Vices*, edited by Kevin Timpe and Craig A. Boyd, 369–91. Oxford: Oxford University Press, 2014.

Zagzebski, Linda. *Virtues of the Mind. An Inquiry into the Nature of Virtue and the Ethical Foundations of Knowledge*. Oxford: Oxford University Press, 1996.